THE
DISCIPLINE
OF
Prayer

by Dr. Dennis Corle
Evangelist, Editor of *Revival Fires!*

Revival Fires! Publishing
P.O. Box 245
Claysburg, PA 16625
(814) 239-2813

printed in the United States of America

CONTENTS

CHAPTER ONE

THE DISCIPLINE OF PRAYER

"And in the morning, rising up a great while before day, he went out, and departed into a solitary place, and there prayed. And Simon and they that were with him followed after him. And when they had found him, they said unto him, All men seek for thee. And he said unto them, Let us go into the next towns, that I may preach there also: for therefore came I forth." (Mark 1:35-38)

There are some things about the life of the Lord Jesus Christ that have to do with who He was. I could never duplicate His perfection. But I can duplicate His consistency and His discipline in some things that He did. I could duplicate some of His practices because discipline is not a miracle. Discipline is a matter of bringing my body into subjection. It is me telling my body what it will do. Most of us allow our bodies to tell us what they are going to do and we respond. Discipline is when I set the boundaries according to the Word of God and tell my body, "This is what we are going to do," and then follow through.

The prayer life of the Lord Jesus illustrates discipline. In our text the Bible says Jesus had the discipline of a set time to commune with His heavenly Father - *"in the morning, rising up a great while before day."* He had a sanctified, or a solitary place to pray - *"he went out...into a solitary place, and there prayed."*

Jesus had some set places where He went for prayer. He had some places set apart for the work of intercession. There are two things you will notice about that place of prayer: (1) it was always a solitary place, where He could get away from the hustle and bustle; and (2) it was always a specific place where He had frequently gone. The disciples knew where to find Him. That tells us something. Would to God you and I were consistent enough about our Christianity that folks would know where to find us at set times.

Jesus had a steady habit. In verses 36 and 37 the fact that His disciples knew where to find Him gives proof of His habitual practice of going to this set place. He did this all the time. This was not a passing fancy for the Lord Jesus. This was a daily activity. If it was that important for Jesus Christ, the Son of God, to have the discipline of a set time, a solitary place, and a steady habit, how much more important is it for frail beings like you and me to exercise the discipline of prayer?

For people to be consistent in the matter of prayer is not natural. There are several things in the Christian life that take discipline. That means that those things do not come naturally. If you and I do not exercise discipline we will not pray, and most folks do not. Soulwinning is a discipline. You will not go soulwinning if you do not schedule soulwinning and plan to go, and make yourself do what you are supposed to do on those days when you are not excited about it.

The Christian life is a disciplined life, telling my body, "This is what the Bible says. This is right. Whether I feel like it or not, we are going to do what the Word of God says, consistently, by schedule, on purpose, not by accident."

It is vital that you and I set a time to pray. If we are going to pray we have to be willing to set a time. It ought to have enough importance to be scheduled. It takes time to commune with God. It takes time to intercede for others. It takes time to pray and do what ought to be done. Time has to be given to prayer.

I think God deserves the best hours of the day, not the leftover moments at night before you crawl into bed, after having operated all day without getting in touch with heaven. God wants the quality time and quiet time, uninterrupted, where you are not involved in a dozen different thought patterns. God would like your attention as well as your time.

Most of the time, when we do pray, we pray with our minds being distracted and other things going on about us. We really are not giving God the attention that He ought to have. We are not giving ourselves to prayer.

We also need to give quantity time to prayer. We sing the song, "Sweet Hour of Prayer." Now, if we sang the truth we would have to sing, "Fleeting moment of prayer, that interrupts my life of care." Having a fervent prayer life is not a reality to most of the people of God. One of the great reasons is because we do not have the discipline of prayer established in our hearts.

A preacher came to John Wesley. He said, "It is rumored that you spend two hours a day in prayer. Is that true?" Wesley said, "Yes, that is true. From four o'clock to six o'clock every morning I pray." The preacher said, "Well, I am just too busy to pray two hours a day." Wesley said to him, "Sir, I am too busy not to pray two hours a day. I cannot get done what has to get done without the help and intervention of God Almighty."

Fervent prayer is not an accident nor is it an incident. It is a discipline of life. It is something that becomes a part of your character. It is something that becomes a good habit. It is something that you ultimately do by reflex and with a hunger for communion with God.

Isn't it amazing how folks talk about not having time to pray? "I know I need to, but I just do not have time to pray?" Isn't it strange that you have time to eat, time to sleep, time to fellowship, time to make money, time to play, but you cannot find time in your busy schedule to commune with the God who breathed this universe into existence? If you and I believe what the Bible says then we ought to think it is important enough to get in touch with God.

Is praying as important as eating? Is it as important as sleeping? Is it as important as making money? Then if I have time for those things, and I schedule those things, I ought to schedule prayer.

When you have a job you set the alarm clock. If you do not get up you will not get paid. You say, "I do not feel like it this morning, but I must get up, and I must go to work. I have a responsibility and I am going to make myself do what I am supposed to do." You need contact with God more than you need all the money you could gather. I am not against making money, but I am for scheduling time for God Almighty and putting Him first. We rush off to the work of the day, and there are so many things that pull on us.

Back a couple of months ago, I had a man staying with me in the motel room. On the Monday that we were going to leave he was in a hurry. He is a newlywed and he wanted to get back and spend some time with his wife. I don't blame him.

I finished my prayer time and I was sitting there reading my Bible. Boy, he wanted to get packed up and get out of there. He was almost upset with me because I was not jumping up and running out the door. He was just pacing the floor. He said, "I am going to go on over to the church. I will wait for you there." I said to him, "Have you prayed yet?" "Well, I was going to do that at the church." I said, "Sure, you are. Have you read your Bible yet." "No." I said, "Look. Start the day with God. The rest of it is going to go smoother if you do."

There was work waiting for him over at the church. There were boxes to load. He got his mind on that before he got his mind on God. God wants to have preeminence in our lives. He certainly does not have preeminence if He does not have space. Certainly, we want to stay in touch with Him all day long. Yes, we want to have communion with Him. But we need to give Him some set time where He has our attention and we commune with Him on purpose.

E.M. Bounds said, "Not to give prayer and religion a set and sacred time is to murder it outright." Some of us are guilty of murder. We did not kill anybody. We killed our prayer time.

Most of us have good intentions. But once you get into the hustle and bustle it is over. Too many things demand your time and attention. They captivate you and keep you from giving God what He deserves.

The devil fears nothing more than he fears prayer. So he fights nothing more fiercely than he fights our prayer lives.

Dr. John Rice said, "Every problem for a child of God is a prayer problem." The truth is that we experience things that we could overcome if we scheduled prayer, if we had the discipline of a set time. To be indefinite about our prayer time, or to give it less than our prime time, is to really not give it respect. It is to slight prayer. It is to say, "Yes, it is a luxury, but not a necessity. It would be a wonderful thing to do if you have time."

Anything that is right to do demands that you schedule it. You do not wait for time to come around. Just tell them at work that when you have time you will show up. Then let everything that grabs for your time and attention keep you from work, and see how long you have a job.

The Bible says that Jesus went out a great while before day. The Psalmist of Israel said, *"Early will I seek thee."* In Acts 3:1 the Bible says that Peter and John went up to the temple at the ninth hour, being the hour of prayer, a scheduled time where they got together to pray. How about that? David said, *"Evening, and morning, and at noon will I pray."* They had scheduled times, set times to get in touch with God.

Daniel knelt in his room with his window open toward Jerusalem seven times a day. The Bible makes it very clear that when God created Adam and Eve and put them into the garden of Eden they walked with God in the cool of the day. Every day there was a scheduled time for walking with God, communing with God.

We have times to eat and times to sleep, but no time to pray. Something is wrong with our priorities. Something is wrong with our discipline of life. The best hours of the day are always the morning hours. They are the most uninterrupted. If God is not first in our thoughts and efforts in the morning, He will be in last place all day long.

The two statements that the Bible makes about Jesus, *"in the morning,"* and *"a great while before day,"* are significant statements. God is trying to teach us something. Nothing in the Bible is there by accident. It is there because God has something for us to learn. So often we miss statements like these, connected to the prayer habit of the Son of God. Morning listlessness is a sign of a cold, indifferent, listless heart. The heart that is slow to seek after God in the morning is a heart that has lost its relish for the person of God. It has lost its appetite and hunger for God Himself.

God is more concerned that you and I fall in love with Him than that we fall in love with His work. He wants us to do His work, but He wants us to love Him first. He wants us to seek Him first.

The disciples came to Jesus and said, *"All men seek thee."* He said, "I know, and I am going to see them in a minute. But I had to get My prayer time taken care of first. I got out here before they got out of bed so I could be ready to minister to them when they came." You and I need to give some time, a set time, to prayer.

Robert Murray McCheyne was a great man of prayer. He tottered into the grave at the ripe old age of twenty-nine. He literally prayed himself to death. Most of us, if we live to be one hundred and twenty-nine, will not accomplish in the extra hundred years what he did in his twenty-nine years of fervent prayer. He said, "A wretched system, and unscriptural it is, not to begin the day seeking God. The morning hours, from six to eight, are the most uninterrupted and should be thus employed."

Francis Asbury, an old circuit riding preacher, had pleurisy so bad that he would have to wrap his body, take a stick and twist it and ride for fifty or sixty miles in some cases in great pain. He said this about his prayer life, "I propose to rise at four o'clock as often as I can, and to spend two hours in prayer and meditation." These men probably went to bed about eight or nine o'clock. You cannot go to bed at two o'clock in the morning and get up at four.

Samuel Rutherford, a great old prayer warrior, said that he rose at three o'clock in the morning to meet God in prayer and did not miss a morning watch. Joseph Elene spent from four o'clock to eight o'clock in prayer and communion with God. Of the noise created by those who rose earlier than he, he would bemoan himself. He said, "This noise shames me greatly. Does not my Master deserve better than theirs?" He said, "I am getting up at four and praying till eight. Somebody gets up at three thirty to make money. That grieves me." Martin Luther said he could do nothing worthwhile if his best three hours had not been spent in prayer.

Have you ever noticed that the people we read about in Christian history were people who knew something about prayer? They had a good work ethic, but they knew something about the discipline of prayer. You read about the lives of meh like Abel Clarey, who traveled with Charles Finney. Charles Finney was probably the greatest revivalist who ever lived since the time of the apostle Paul. Finney said, "On many occasions my reward most likely will be given to a man by the name of Abel Clarey, who would literally pray by the hour and by the day in private." Sometimes that old man would pour out his soul in intercessory prayer for eight or ten hours a day, laboring, and never even show up at the meeting. But the mighty power of God would fall.

David Brainerd was another man who tottered into the grave at the ripe old age of twenty-nine. He died in the house of Jonathan Edwards, the man who preached "Sinners in the Hands of an Angry God" and began the Great Awakening in the Northeast. As David Brainerd was dying, Edwards said, "I thank God that in His providence He allowed Brainerd to die in my home that I might hear his prayers and see his compassion and hear his intercession." It affected his life.

John Hyde was known as Praying Hyde, the apostle of prayer, and "the man who never sleeps," because of his constant interceding for others, his constant prayer. These men were dedicated to prayer. They knew something about it. There was the power of God that was so real in their every action, in their every move.

David Brainerd said, "I love to be alone at my cottage where I can spend much time in prayer." Most folks do not know much about spending much time in prayer. Most folks do not have the discipline of a set time. God is not important enough for them to schedule time for Him. Prayer is not measured by moments alone, but to give only a few moments to it is a sign of disrespect.

I have preacher boys travel with me every summer. Every morning I make them turn in a devotional report of how many chapters of the Bible they read and how much time they spent in prayer. One day I looked at their reports. One young man had prayed three minutes that morning. One had prayed ten minutes. One had prayed five, one had prayed twelve. The whole bunch of them together had not prayed an hour. I said, "Fellas, all eight of you did not spend enough time in prayer for one good man of God."

Let me ask you a question. How much time did you spend in prayer this morning? What if we collected your report?

I remember reading about John Welsh. He spent seven or eight hours a day in prayer. You say, "Well, I do not think I could do that." Do you think maybe you could spend forty-five minutes? Do you think maybe you could find half an hour for God somewhere? Do you think maybe He could get important enough in your life where you thought it was important to schedule a set time to meet Him every day?

Our laziness after God is the crying sin of this day. We are so carnal and worldly in our thinking. Even the cleanest-living people, the most religious people, are so out of touch with the matter of prayer and communion with a holy God. The children of the world pursue their desires early and late and in between, while the people of God neither pursue Him early nor late, and their midday pursuit of God is tame and feeble at best.

E.M. Bounds said, "No man gets God in His fulness

who does not follow hard after Him, and no man follows hard after God who is not after Him before the day dawns." Oh, for the discipline of a set time and plenty of it, early, before the hustle and bustle of the day, before the distractions of life, before all the things that seek our attention.

We need the discipline of a sanctified, solitary place. Jesus went out into a solitary place. The fact that the disciples knew where to find Him tells us that He had some places that He frequented. There were some places where He had prayed before. The Bible talks about the Mount of Olives, where He oft resorted to prayer. There were some places that were sacred to the Son of God. There were some meeting places that were set apart, where He did nothing but get in touch with His heavenly Father consistently.

He went to a place where there was no distraction. He got away from the work so He could get in touch with His heavenly Father. In Matthew chapter seven Jesus gave us some instruction in prayer. He said, *"When ye pray, enter into your closet."* He was talking about a private place, a secluded place, a place of no distractions. In Acts chapter ten the Bible says that Peter went to a housetop to pray. Everybody else was down there fellowshiping and Peter went up and confined himself to pray.

Your prayer place ought to be a sanctified place, a place that is sacred to you. It ought to have some atmosphere to it. The first time you pray someplace there is nothing sacred about it. But after you have prevailed with God somewhere, once the mighty power of God falls on your life there, once you see God meet your need there, once the answer comes, there will be something about that place. I am talking about a place that is given to the work of prayer only. I am talking about a place that makes us think of God and past wrestlings, times that we have prevailed. I am talking about a place that refreshes our memory, a place that warms our affections, a place that quickens our faith.

Real prayer has not only to do with the act of crying out to God, but it has something to do with an atmosphere. If you are distracted by other things, you are not going to have the atmosphere that makes prayer what it ought to be.

Bethel may have just been an ordinary place to everyone else, but it was not just another place to Jacob. He had prevailed there. He had become a prince with God and man there. We need to have a place like that.

That holy mount was a special place to Moses. He had met with God there numerous times. He had consistently gotten in touch with God there. He had seen the Shekinah glory there.

Jesus had His mount of Olives. Daniel had his chamber that faced Jerusalem where he prayed seven times a day. John Wesley had his little closet where he so consistently prayed that he literally wore grooves into the floor with his knees. David Brainerd had his secluded cottage where he went to pray. William Bramwell, a mighty man of prayer, had his favorite forest, into the depths of which he went to meet with God. John Fletcher, the old Methodist, had a little room where he spent so much time that he literally stained the walls of the room with the breath of his prayers. Charles Finney had a place in the woods, where shortly after his conversion he entered and came out of that place the same day, filled with the Holy Ghost of God. In his later years he went there frequently to commune with his God.

Samuel Rutherford could say of a wooded, consecrated spot where he had prayed, "There wrestled I with the angel of the Lord and prevailed." You read about the life of Ford Porter, a modern day prayer warrior. He went to heaven just a few years ago. He had a little attic area where he daily prayed for hours.

To fail to give prayer a set time and a sanctified place is to despise the very act of prayer. It is to lightly esteem it.

Stop and think about this. What is the kitchen for? Oh, that is the eating place. What is the bedroom for? That is the sleeping place. Do you have a shower in the bathroom, or do you bathe outside? Isn't it a strange thing how that you have a special place where you eat, you have a special place where you sleep, you have a special place where you bathe? You not only have a set time, you have a set room for it. There is a place set up to do that one thing. That room is sanctified to that one purpose. Isn't it amazing that we do not have a special place to get in touch with God in prayer? Does that tell you anything?

No wonder Paul said to Titus about some of those folks, " Their god is their belly." All they thought about were the carnal things. Those things were important. They had set times and set places for everything that was temporary, and no time and no place for the things that are eternal.

The habitual place of prayer, that place where you come again, and again, and again, will kindle a livelier faith and a stronger ardor for God. It will elevate your feelings and fix your concentration on the things of God. There is something about that atmosphere.

When I come into the kitchen and sit down I am ready to eat. There is something about the atmosphere, not just the time. When I go into a restaurant and sit down I do not want to wait three hours to eat. I am ready. When I go to bed I do not toss and turn. I am ready to sleep.

I have a time and place for everything I do. If Christianity is ever going to have a great effect on you and those around you, it has to be important enough to have time and place in your life.

We need the discipline of a steady habit. The disciples knew where to find Jesus. That is because they found Him there before. He had shown them those places before. They were places of prayer. They knew what to expect of Him because He not only had good habits, He had godly habits.

In Luke 22:39 the Bible says, *"And he came out, and went as he was wont..."* That word 'wont' means He had a habit of doing it. 'As he did aforetime.' 'As He did frequently.' It was a reflex, habitual action, that He had done over and over again. This text deals with prayer. *"And he came out, and went as he was wont to the mount of Olives; and his disciples also followed him...And he was withdrawn from them about a stone's cast, and kneeled down, and prayed."*

God gives us the discipline of a steady habit in the life of the Lord Jesus. He was not hit and miss, on and off, up and down. He was not sometimes there and sometimes not. He had a steady habit of doing the things that He ought to do. That is how Judas knew where to find Him on that night. He was at the mount of Olives, where He always was at night, to pray.

Negligence and inconsistency are two of the greatest enemies of Christianity. We talk about all of the wicked sins in people's lives, but we do more damage by negligence and inconsistency than by all of the other things compounded. E.M. Bounds said, "The surest way to kill religion is not to murder it outright, but to kill it piecemeal, to allow other interests, even the most pressing and benevolent, to crowd out our religious duties. To crowd them into a corner is to kill them slowly but surely." If you squeeze prayer in, it will get squeezed out more often than not. If you squeeze it in it is because you do not have a set time. If you squeeze it in it is because you do not have a set place. If you squeeze it in it is because you have not set out to establish a steady, consistent habit.

Habits are things that become reflex. A fella that has a smoking habit reaches into his pocket without thinking. I was preaching in Arkansas one night. I looked over, and this woman was about to light up a cigarette in the church until someone reached over and got her by the arm. She forgot where she was.

I was on a commuter airplane. There was a woman who had never flown before two seats away from me, just shaking like a leaf. You are not allowed to smoke in any of those little planes, even back before they made the no smoking laws on flights. She got out her cigarette and lit it up. The pilot looked back and said, "Hey, put that out." She said, "Oh, I didn't know I had it lit." What happened? It was reflex. When she got nervous she just reached for a cigarette. She had done it so many times before that she did not even think about it. It was a habit.

God wants you and me to schedule things consistently enough and do them faithfully enough that they become reflex actions to us. If you can develop bad habits, it is also possible for you to develop good ones. If somebody can develop a bad habit of drinking booze and smoking cigarettes and using snuff, somebody could develop a good habit of reading their Bible and praying and telling people about Jesus. It is possible.

In Daniel chapter six the Bible says Daniel prayed as he did aforetime. That was after they had made a bad law and said he could not pray anymore. He said, "I was not planning on praying any more, but I am not praying any less, either. I am just going to do it like I always did it."

Those who have been known as great heroes of the faith in years gone by are people who had a steady habit of prayer. They tell me it takes thirty-nine days to develop a habit. If you do the same thing at the same time the same way every day for thirty-nine days it will become a reflex action. You will do it without thinking about it. Most of us have never had a thirty-nine day prayer habit, with a set time and a sanctified place in our entire Christian life. Most of us have never gone thirty-nine days straight where we at the same time and the same place met God for the same purpose without missing in our whole Christian life. Wouldn't it be a wonderful thing if you and I did this so consistently in the morning it became reflex to us?

When I was lost and I smoked cigarettes I used to reach for one before my eyes were fully open in the morning. I had to have a cigarette. I would wake up craving a cigarette, reaching without even thinking, half awake. If I reached over and the pack was empty I was out of bed and on the way to the store. Wouldn't it be a wonderful thing if you ever got to the place where you woke up in the morning and said, "I have to get to the prayer closet. I have to get in touch with God"? Wouldn't it be good if you ever got to the place where you were addicted to the matter of prayer, you had a habit of prayer, an appetite for prayer and a yearning to get in touch with God?

It would be a wonderful thing if you addicted yourself to God. The Bible says the house of Stephanus addicted themselves to the ministry. It does not say they got addicted. It did not happen to them. They happened to it. They did something so consistently that they addicted themselves. If you and I would have enough discipline to set a time, and sanctify a place, and on purpose be there every day for thirty-nine days, it just might be that we would addict ourselves to prayer and communing with God. We might just wake up with a craving for Him. We might just wake up and say, "I have to have Him. I have to have Him."

It is possible for people to be addicted to the will of God and have a craving to do the right thing. I cannot duplicate the perfection of Christ, but I can duplicate His discipline. I cannot duplicate the supernatural in the life of Christ, but I can duplicate the natural discipline that He exercised - the discipline of a set time, a solitary place, and a steady, consistent habit.

I am not going to try to tell you what time makes you spiritual, whether it is four o'clock, or five o'clock or six o'clock. I am not going to try to tell you how much time makes you spiritual. But you ought to start the day, on purpose, with God. Set a place and set a time. Set something that is realistic, something that you can actually live with, and then make up your mind to stick with it. It may be somewhat of a sacrifice. You may have to get up a little earlier than usual. Do not try to be John Wesley overnight. Just set a time, a time you can live with, but where you on purpose meet with God. Sanctify a place. It will not be long until it becomes a special place. Then decide that you are going to discipline yourself to do it every day whether you feel like it or not.

If you will do that for thirty-nine days, have a set time, a sanctified place, and a steady habit, making yourself show up there on purpose, you would be shocked at what it would do to you and how it would transform and excite your prayer life.

A lot of people do not like to come to church because they are not comfortable. They do not know anybody there. Do you know why folks do not like to go to the prayer closet? They do not know Anybody there. They are not comfortable there. Do you know how you get comfortable in a church? You come long enough when you do not know anybody until you meet some folks and get acquainted, until you feel some warmth and some connection there. Do you know how you can get to where you get excited about coming to the prayer closet? When you are cold, and do not feel like it, and do not really have any sweet communion with God, you come and make yourself do what you are supposed to do. Discipline yourself until you establish a sweet communion and relationship with God Almighty.

There was a time when I did not like to go to church. But there is nothing now I like to do more than to be with the people of God. There was a time I really did not like to pray. But I really do like to pray. I have spent enough time with God through the years and seen God do enough things in me, and through me, and for me that now I get excited about prayer.

We are building a house right now. That house is an answer to prayer. God is building that house. God is supplying the money. He is raising up the workers. I have not paid anybody labor. It is all volunteer help, most of it preachers and Christians and churches. Some folks have done the job and supplied the material when they did it. I did not ask them to. I asked God to take care of it. It is amazing what God can do. God is doing some things that I could never do in the flesh. I get excited about that. I have prevailed with God. I think I'll just go ahead and do it again. I have come to the prayer closet and seen God answer before. I am going to come back again.

It is a wonderful thing to be in tune with heaven and in touch with God. You can get addicted to it, and you should.

The discipline of prayer is lacking today. Discipline in general is lacking in people's lives. We have good people, clean people, but discipline is lacking in their lives. We are an undisciplined generation. We are not necessarily wicked, but the best of us are undisciplined. We are inconsistent. We are negligent. We do not set a time. We do not set a place, and we do not work at developing a steady habit to where prayer becomes an addiction, a reflex action. God help us to decide today that we are going to set a time. Decide today. Sit down and determine what time you are going to meet with God. Why don't you decide where there is a quiet place that you can get alone with God? Why don't you get your calendar and decide that you are not going to miss, not for anything, and just mark off thirty-nine days. Do not miss one single time for thirty-nine days.

I think by the time you get through the thirty-nine days that nobody will have to motivate you. Would you try that? Will you cultivate the disciplined habit of prayer?

CHAPTER TWO

PRAYER CHANGES THINGS

"And when they had prayed, the place was shaken where they were assembled together; and they were all filled with the Holy Ghost, and they spake the word of God with boldness." (Acts 4:31)

Prior to this prayer meeting we catch a glimpse of a discouraged, fearful band of believers stifled by the persecuting religious mobs. After this prayer meeting we find an army of Spirit-filled soldiers of the cross going forth in the power of the Holy Spirit, conquering and to conquer. The result was much the same as that which followed a ten day prayer meeting in the first and second chapters of Acts: Pentecostal Power. Not tongues, but power. Power to stand in the face of opposition, power to witness boldly, power to overcome temptation and fear, power to convince the skeptic, and power to bring sinners to Christ.

Prayer is the powerhouse of the church. No Christian is better than his prayer life. The time and fervency spent in supplication to God are indicators of our true spiritual condition.

Prayer changes things. Political involvement is vain without prayer. Human endeavor is useless without prayer. Prayer is the medium by which we lay hold of the power and promises of God Almighty. Prayer changes the pray-er as well as his circumstances.

In 1867, Moody took his wife to England for the sake of her health, and his plain American ways stole the hearts of the British people. When he returned to London in 1872 to learn more about the Bible from that city's great preachers, one pastor persuaded him to speak in his church. During the Sunday morning service, no one seemed interested in the sermon. That night, great change seemed to have come over the congregation. When he gave the invitation, hundreds rose from their seats. Thinking they had misunderstood him, he explained again what he meant. The response was the same. For ten more days, Moody kept preaching in that church, and hundreds of people found Christ. "I wanted to know what this meant," Moody said later. "I began making inquiries and never rested until I found a bed-ridden girl praying that God would bring me to that church. God heard her prayers, and brought me over four thousand miles of land and sea in answer to her request." That girl was Marianne Adlard. Confined to bed by a painful disease, she was unable to attend the services of her church. She had read about Mr. Moody's work with the children in Chicago and prayed earnestly that God would send Moody to London. When she heard that he had come and had preached the morning service at her church, she prayed all afternoon, and that evening revival was God's answer. She continued to pray for Mr. Moody every day after that until his death in 1899.

May we hunger with those of old who cried out, "Lord, teach us to pray!" May we learn the art of soul-stirring supplication that reaches the heart of God. May we realize the value and importance of effectual prayer in our everyday lives...Because Prayer Changes Things.

CHAPTER THREE

ARE YOU GETTING YOUR PRAYERS ANSWERED?

"And this is the confidence that we have in him, that, if we ask any thing according to his will, he heareth us: And if we know that he hear us, whatsoever we ask, we know that we have the petitions that we desired of him." (I John 5:14-15)

This is the confidence, the assurance, the security that we have *in Him.* If God hears us, He answers us. But I have to be in *in Him.* I must be saved in order to have the right to come to God as my Father and expect Him to meet my needs. *"If we ask any thing according to His will He heareth us."* The word 'hear' in the Bible does not just mean that it goes in my ear and I physically hear. It indicates 'to hear with the intent to obey or respond'. We find in Romans 10:17, *"So then faith cometh by hearing, and hearing by the word of God."* That does not mean that I heard a verse and suddenly I have faith. But when I hear with the intent to obey, it produces faith.

When we read *"He heareth us...",* it means that God listens with the intent to respond. If I am in the will of God and praying in the will of God, then I have the confidence that God hears me, and if He hears me with the intent to respond, I have complete confidence that He will do what I ask. I will get my prayers answered. We make all kinds of excuses for not getting our prayers answered. There are a few reasons why we do not, but they are not the reasons we use. I want to ask you, Preacher, are you getting your prayers answered? Ma'am, are you getting your prayers answered? Sir, are you getting your prayers answered? Teenager, are you getting your prayers answered?

I did not ask, "Are you praying?" You may pray an hour or two hours a day. But are you getting any answers? We do need to learn to spend hours in prayer, but I am asking about the **results** of your prayer life. There is no value in talking if no one hears. If my prayers are not being heard, it would not matter if I spent eight hours a day in prayer. I heard a preacher say that the man who got America back to prayer would be the one responsible for revival in America, and I believe that is true. You will not pray without going soulwinning, because you cannot spend much time with God without it moving you to reach those Christ gave His life for - those you are praying for.

Jesus warned his disciples not to be like the scribes and the Pharisees. *"But when ye pray, use not vain repetitions, as the heathen do: for they think that they shall be heard for their much speaking."* *(Matthew 6:7)* You say, "I pray three hours a day." You ought to get a set of rosary beads if you are just putting in the time. In I Kings chapter eighteen, Elijah needed a big answer from God. Surely he must have prayed for several hours.

No, his prayer was just sixty-three words but the fire of God fell and consumed the sacrifice, the water, the wood, the stone and the dust, and caused the people to say, *"The LORD, He is the God."* If you ever got a prayer answered, the folks around you might say the same thing. If some of you ever got a prayer answered, it would shock everybody you know. If some of you ever got a prayer answered, it would shock YOU. As a matter of fact, if some of you ever prayed, it would shock God!

Dr. John Rice often said, "Every Christian ought to experience daily answers to prayer." Do not tell me about the prayer you got answered sixteen years ago, back when you prayed and lived clean enough for God to hear you. What prayers did you get answered today or yesterday? George Mueller cited over one hundred thousand definite answers to prayer in his lifetime. I like what it says about Jesus in John 11:41. *"And Jesus lifted up his eyes, and said, Father, I thank thee that thou hast heard me. And I knew that thou hearest me always"* I am glad He is my Intercessor. He always gets His prayers answered. Jesus is always on praying ground.

I believe that one of the curses of our generation is the lack of keeping a prayer list or diary. Years ago I traveled with Dr. Joe Boyd. He always kept a prayer list, and when he got an answer he would write 'TUG' beside that item - "Thank You, God." So that is what I began to do. In the past several weeks I have put more TUG's on there than you could shake a stick at. I am talking about three thousand dollar answers to prayer. God will probably never give me any money because He knows I would get so backslidden I would not pray. This ministry could not exist without daily answers to prayer.

On one occasion I was in a laundromat in North Carolina with my wife, and I witnessed to an old hippie guy. He said, "Christianity is just a crutch." I said, "Let me ask you a question." He was all set for some theological or scientific question. I said, "I just have one question. If there is nothing to Christianity, and the Bible is not true and God is non-existent, I want you to explain how I have had seventy definite answers to prayer in the last ninety days. "Well," he said, "that is a coincidence." I asked, "How many coincidences did you have in the last ninety days?"

We were traveling in a motor home and praying for a small car we could tow. I was out soulwinning with a pastor and he asked me, "How do you like this car?" I said, "This is really nice." He said, "You could probably use one like this, couldn't you?" I said, "Yes, I probably could." He said, "My wife and I believe that God wants us to give you this car." Brother, God answers prayer!

We talk more about prayer and do less actual praying than any generation that has ever lived in this country. We all know about Jonathan Edwards' famous message: Sinners In The Hands Of An Angry God. That message shook the northeastern United States and started the Great Awakening which lasted for twenty years. One fifth of the inhabitants of the American colonies were born again during that twenty year period.

Everyone raves about the sermon, and indeed it was a mighty message, but the key to those results was not in the preaching. Edwards leaned up against the pulpit because of his poor eyesight, and read the manuscript in a monotone with not one gesture, but people grabbed the supporting beams and screamed, "Help us, we are sliding into hell."

What most people do not know is that for three days and three nights prior to stepping into the pulpit Jonathan Edwards had not had any food or sleep. He spent those three days and nights primarily in prayer. He was heard crying out repeatedly, "Oh, God, give me New England." They said that when he stepped into the pulpit, it was as though he had gazed into the very face of God. Where is that kind of praying in our day?

We do not know anything today about supplication or travail of soul. I do not believe that you 'pray through' in order to be saved. But I think that when it comes to getting prayers answered, they were a lot closer to the truth that you have to be able to get a hold of God. Again, I am not talking about travailing to get saved, but to get answers. Getting saved is as simple as trusting

Christ. You do not even have to move your lips to get saved. I have never seen anything like this generation of preachers fighting over semantics and terminology. Words, words, words. Trust Christ, that will save you, and you can word it any way you want.

Jonathan Edwards asked God to do a mighty work and He did. Prayer affects eternity and moves the hand of God. The Bible says that if we pray in the will of God, we know that He hears us, and if we know He hears us, we know we have the petitions we desired of Him.

Prayer has played a vital role throughout the history of America. Prayer guided Columbus to the New World in 1492. In 1620, prayer brought the Pilgrims to safety and religious liberty. Prayer, in 1623, saved the Pilgrim fathers from starvation. In 1777, at Valley Forge, prayer saved the Continental army and won the war for American independence. While the English general was playing cards, Washington was on his knees, and the inferior army, with the help of God, was the victor.

Prayer, in Philadelphia, saved the Constitutional Convention and gave birth to the American way of life. Prayer, in 1857, saved America from economic destruction. Prayer, in 1918, ended World War I. These infidels and in-for-hell's can say anything they want to about prayer, but this country was born in the prayer closet. The history books make villains out of our Christian heroes, and leave out the fact that prayer entered in to every major event in our history. America is drowning in a quagmire of sin because we have forgotten how to pray. Our kids will not learn anything about prayer unless we teach them. But why are we not getting our prayers answered?

Many of us are not having answered prayer because of sin in our lives. *"If I regard iniquity in my heart, the Lord will not hear me." (Psalm 66:18)* This is about sin in our hearts, and often we are guilty of sin people can not see. It could be bitterness or gossip or self-righteousness. We have a lot of Pharisees in fundamentalism. We say, "If your sin is like my sin, you are okay. But if you have ever been guilty of something I have not done, you are horribly bad." I am not advocating the lowering of Bible standards or a lack of separation. I am talking about compassion and believing that the blood of Christ really does cleanse from all sin. When God forgets it, we ought to forget it.

Some of us do not get our prayers answered because we are so self-righteous and judgmental that God cannot bless us. We are so preoccupied with, "Who is qualified to do this, and who is qualified to do that," that we are not even qualified to get our prayers answered. "God could not use so-and-so because..." Who appointed you as God anyway? It looks to me like God is using some of these people that cannot be used. Some of them are getting more people saved and more prayers answered that you are. God hears everything that goes on, even what you think. But if I regard iniquity in my heart, the Lord will not *hear* me with the intent to respond.

What about God's promise of revival? *"If my people, which are called by my name, shall humble themselves, and pray, and seek my face, and turn from their wicked ways; then will I hear from heaven, and will forgive their sin, and will heal their land."* If we want to see revival, we will have to turn from our wicked ways, then He will hear and forgive and heal. We talk about the grace of God, and then hold grudges and bitterness and self-righteousness, and we have bad attitudes. I would rather run with someone who may be slightly off in doctrine than to spend time around preachers and Christians who have a nasty spirit. Mistaken doctrine is not nearly as un-Christlike as a hateful, vengeful, stinking attitude. I am convinced God cannot bless us because we have become the elite group. We know it all and we sit in judgment, looking down our long, Pharisaical noses. If I am sick of it, I wonder how God feels?

We have to turn from *our* wicked ways. Long hair on men, britches on women and X-rated movies are not the only things that are wrong. But some of you are doing those things, too. It was confusing for my children when they were small. We have convictions. My girls wear knee-length dresses and culottes, and that is what they swim in, too. We feel the same way about running around in a bathing suit as we feel about running around in underwear. We pull into some of these churches and here comes the pastor's wife in a pair of pants, his son has long hair, and the kids are running around in shorts and swimsuits. My kids ask, "Are they saved?" I try to teach my kids to respect preachers, but I do not want them to lower their standards to do it. I have to say, "They just do not believe what the Bible says about it, honey."

"Well, you are a legalist!" Then so is God. He put fruit in the Garden of Eden and said, "Do not touch it." As soon as you say something is wrong, you are a legalist. You would not know a legalist if you stumbled over one. Legalism is adding to the plan of salvation like the Catholics and the Church of Christ and the tongues-speakers. You get saved by grace through faith, but after you get saved right is still right and wrong is still wrong, and if you intend to please God, you are going to have to obey His Word.

Did you know that secret sins are no secret to God? Sin in our hearts will keep us from getting our prayers answered. I guarantee you that there are preachers who have sin in their lives and they know it. There are moms and dads and teenagers who have sin in their lives and nobody knows it but them and God, but you cannot get your prayers answered.

The second reason why you cannot get your prayers answered is that you ask amiss. The Bible says, *"Ye have not because ye ask not."* Then it says,*"Ye ask, and receive not, because ye ask amiss, that ye may consume it upon your lusts"* *(James 4:3)*. Nothing lies beyond the reach of prayer but that which lies beyond the will of God. We sometimes ask for things that are outside the will of God, and God will not respond because it is not right or it is not best for us. We sometimes ask for things that would hurt us spiritually. Many things, if we would pray long enough and fervently enough for, God could one day give us, because in that time spent praying we would grow spiritually to the point that we could handle what we are asking for. But we do not pray enough, and God says, "No, that will hurt you. You are not mature enough for that yet."

We ask for what we cannot handle, and we ask for our pleasure instead of God's glory. In Psalm 50:15 we read, *"And call upon me in the day of trouble: I will deliver thee, and thou shalt glorify me."* Answered prayer is to glorify God. It is not wrong for me to pray for my needs to be met. But it is wrong for my motive to be just for my needs to be met. I need to learn to pray for the glory and praise of God. Folks that use God for a spare tire would not understand what I am talking about. The only time you want to be bothered with God is when you have a flat. If your purpose is to serve and glorify God, it will be reflected in your prayer life.

If I have the mind of Christ, then God can give me everything I ask for, because I will only want what I ought to have and what will please God. Too many preachers are trying to build a name for themselves and be 'somebody'. You know, God never makes 'somebody' out of somebody who wants to be 'somebody'. If you would just get head-over-heels in love with Jesus and be willing to be a nobody for His glory, you would be somebody and not even know it.

As a preacherboy, I went to the Southwide Baptist Fellowship with Dr. Boyd. After the service one night a couple of well known preachers said, "Hey, Joe. Do you want to go out with us to get something to eat?" He said, "I have this preacherboy with me..." He fished around to see if there was an invitation for me. One of them said, "Oh, he can probably find something out in the bus, can't he?" Brother Boyd said, "Well, I don't guess I will go tonight. Maybe some other time." I have never forgotten this. As soon as those big name preachers walked out the door, he put his arm around my shoulder and said, "Come on, son. Let's go get something to eat."

I am so weary of big-shot politicians in fundamentalism. No wonder we do not have a generation of young men coming up to stand in the gap. We would not give them the time of day because they are not famous. Real men of God have a heart for young preachers. I would just as soon hear a young preacherboy with his heart on fire as anybody I have ever heard in my life. You "big shots" need to love them before they get so full of theology that they do not believe in 'knee-ology' anymore. Some of us do not get our prayers answered because we ask amiss.

There is another reason why we do not get our prayers answered. Our marriages and our homes are not right. *"For after this manner in the old time the holy women also, who trusted in God, adorned themselves, being in subjection unto their own husbands: Even as Sara obeyed Abraham, calling him lord: whose daughters ye are, as long as ye do well, and are not afraid with any amazement. Likewise, ye husbands, dwell with them according to knowledge, giving honour unto the wife, as unto the weaker vessel, and as being heirs together of the grace of life; that your prayers be not hindered."* If our homes are out of order and we willfully disobey God's principles about our homes, we will not get our prayers answered.

Ladies are supposed to submit and obey their husbands as much as they are to obey the Lord. Men are supposed to honor and cherish their wives, loving them sacrificially and unselfishly as Christ loved the church. Some of you have children who are unsaved or in the world, and they desperately need you to be able to get your prayers answered, but you refuse to have a Bible-centered home and do your part to obey God in a scriptural marriage.

God's plan is for a heaven-on-earth with the man as the leader and the woman following. When I say leader, I do not mean tyrant. *"As Christ loved the church..."* That is how you are supposed to love your wife. Is Jesus a tyrant? Is He unreasonable, lazy or selfish? We have people who pray for their children every day and cannot get an answer, because husbands and wives will not get right with God and right with each other. ERA was spawned in hell, but if it were not for this generation of men with a string for a backbone and baloney for brains, it would never have happened. Your home needs a godly, loving leader.

I heard a joke that reminded me of this 'out-of-control' situation. There was a wreck in Mississippi, and the police officer who arrived on the scene found the man, woman and two children all unconscious. He waited around a few minutes, and felt that he ought to do something about his accident report. A pet monkey was jumping around inside the car, so he decided to ask him a few questions. The officer pointed to the man and asked, "What was he doing?" The monkey held an imaginary bottle up, tilted his head back and went, "Glug-glug-glug". "He was drinking, right?" The monkey nodded his head in agreement.

"What was she doing?" the policeman inquired, pointing at the woman. The monkey made jabbering motions with his fingers and said, "Yap - yap - yap." "Oh, she must have been nagging," the officer realized. Again the monkey nodded his agreement. The officer wrote that down, then looked up and pointed to the children. "And what were they doing?" The monkey clenched his fists and boxed at the air. "Oh, they were fighting." Vigorously, the monkey nodded. The officer felt he had really succeeded after all, so he put his pen in his pocket, folded his report, and said, "By the way, what were you doing?" The monkey clenched his invisible steering wheel and said, "Varoom-varoom." Most of our homes are run by a bunch of humanists who think they are monkeys. No wonder they are a wreck!

Our homes need to be in order and our relationships within the home ought to be loving and scriptural. God stressed the vital importance of proper family relationships by saying *"that your prayers be not hindered."*

Another reason why we cannot get their prayers answered is because we are not winning souls. Jesus said, *"I am the vine, ye are the branches: He that abideth in me, and I in him, the same bringeth forth much fruit: for without me ye can do nothing."* *(John 15:7)* The fruit of the Christian is not love, joy, peace, longsuffering, gentleness, goodness, faith, meekness and temperance. That is the fruit of the Holy Spirit in a Christian's life. His fruit enables me to bear my fruit. It gives me what I need to be an effective soulwinner. *'The fruit of the righteous is a tree of life; and he that winneth souls is wise."* (Proverbs 11:30) He did not say that the fruit of the righteous is another piece of fruit, but a fruit-bearing tree - another soulwinning Christian.

In John chapter fifteen He said if I would abide in Him, I would bear much fruit. Then in verse seven He said, *'If ye abide in me, and my words abide in you, ye shall ask what ye will, and it shall be done unto you."* If you are abiding in Christ you will be winning souls and getting your prayers answered. In verse sixteen He again links prayer and soulwinning. *'Ye have not chosen me, but I have chosen you, and ordained you, that ye should go and bring forth fruit, and that your fruit should remain: that whatsoever ye shall ask of the Father in my name, he may give it you."* It says that if we bear fruit God *may* give us what we ask. God has prohibited himself from answering prayer for people who are fruitless and refuse to try to bear fruit.

I am not talking about your ability nearly as much as your concern. I preached on soulwinning and a little lady about eighty-five years old came forward and said she wanted to be a soulwinner. That afternoon she went out. When she came back to the service that night, she said, "Harry and I did not win anybody but we witnessed to a whole bunch of them." Both of them were out there walking with canes. You cannot reach someone else's potential, but God knows what yours is.

Did you ever notice that the same people who are great soulwinners are also great prayer warriors. Was Jonathan Edwards a great prayer warrior? Was he a great soulwinner? How about Spurgeon, and Finney, and Moody, and Sunday? How about John Rice and Jack Hyles and Joe Boyd? Great soulwinners are great prayer warriors and great prayer warriors are great soulwinners because they are abiding in Christ. Abiding in Christ produces soulwinning and answered prayer - always.

Because we have sin in our lives, because we pray amiss, because our family lives are wrong, because we are not winning souls -- those are all reasons why people do not get their prayers answered. But some of us, to the very best of our knowledge, have those things in order. Then why are we not getting our prayers answered? Because we quit praying too soon. *"Ask, and it shall be given you: seek, and ye shall find; knock and it shall be opened unto you: For every one that asketh receiveth; and he that seeketh findeth; and to him that knocketh it shall be opened."* (*Matthew 7:7-8*) That 'ask' is a durative word that means 'ask and keep on asking, seek and keep on seeking, knock and keep on knocking, and God will surely answer.'

You see, God expects us to spend some hours alone with Him travailing in prayer to become enough like Him to handle the answers that He wants to give us. But we are not equipped to handle them and we do not pray. Some of you guys praying for a thousand in Sunday School could not handle a thousand. But if you will spend the time in prayer alone with God, pleading and getting to know Him, He will equip you and then He will give you that answer. D. L. Moody said that most prayers are like little boys who knock on doors at Halloween and run before anyone answers. They are just an aggravation.

"Well, Lord, if it be Your will, and You are not too busy today, and You do not mind, and..." We come to God in prayer, but we have never seen Him answer one before, so why should we expect one this time? We spend two or three minutes saying, "Dear Lord, Please meet all our needs and God bless everybody." If you got an answer you would never know it. We need to learn to come to God and get on our faces. The Bible says that Daniel got on his face and for twenty-one days pleaded with God. When the angel arrived with the answer, he said, "Daniel, the day you started praying we left heaven, but we got into this battle and the devil held us up in getting here." Twenty-one days later Daniel was still on his face begging God and expectantly awaiting the answer.

We give up too easily. We are a generation of quitters. We have become satisfied with failure. I have said it again and again: You show me a good loser, and I will show you a loser. I think you ought to have a Christian attitude, but it ought to bother you to lose, and especially when you are in a battle with the devil. I have never gotten to the place where I am a good loser. I cannot stand to lose anything. Do not quit! Do not quit!

We give up too soon in prayer. We do not want it bad enough. We are not willing to pay the price. We will not travail in the prayer closet. We do not know anything about fasting. Samuel Chadwick said, "Have you any days of fasting? Have you any nights of prayer as Christ did?" We make major decisions and then split and splinter everything we have to undo them. If Jesus prayed all night before He chose the twelve, what makes you think that we can afford to make decisions without spending time on our faces before God?

Some would have you to believe that the days of miraculous answers to prayer are over. In Genesis chapter eighteen the impossible took place. The angel of the Lord told Abraham and Sarah that He would give them a son. Here they are, old and withered, years beyond the age of childbearing. Sarah was ninety years old and Abraham was nearly one hundred. When Sarah heard them she laughed. The angel asked her this question: *"Is anything too hard for the Lord?"* He told her, *"At the appointed time I will return."* Nothing is too hard for God, but I am going to have to wait until the appointed time. I will have to keep praying and believing and trusting and begging God.

In April of 1912 a lady was oppressed with fear and unable to sleep. Her husband was aboard a ship called the Titanic. She rose in the wee hours of the morning and paced the floor, troubled and fearful. God impressed her heart with the need to pray, and she got on her knees and pleaded with God on her husband's behalf, having no idea of his whereabouts or condition. She stayed on her knees in earnest supplication until five o'clock in the morning, when God gave her a peace in her soul that the crisis was past. She rose from her knees, got into bed, and slept like a baby.

At the same time that she was praying, her husband, Colonel Gracey, was out amidst those icy waters, working frantically to load women and children into the lifeboats. He had given up all hope of his own rescue. As he worked, his heart broke with desire to say goodbye to his dear wife. He cried out into the night, "Goodbye, my darling." They shoved the last lifeboat away and the whirlpool sucked him down with the ship. With no real hope, he instinctively began to swim. Within moments he surfaced beside a lifeboat that had been turned over. He crawled into the lifeboat with others who were holding on to the sides. It was precisely at five o'clock in the morning that a ship stopped and took them aboard to safety.

That little woman could get her prayers answered in the life and death crisis of a loved one. Can you? I wonder, if someone you loved dearly was in danger, and their life depended upon it, could you get your prayers answered? If a loved one was lost, and their salvation depended totally on your prayer life, could you get your prayers answered? If you faced the greatest tragedy of your life today, could you get your prayers answered?

Let us put aside the facade and veneer, and quit trying to impress each other and get down to where we live. How is your church doing? How is your family doing? Are you getting your prayers answered? Maybe it is because of sin. Maybe it is because you have been asking amiss. Maybe it is because you have not been praying at all. Maybe it is because your marriage relationship is wrong. Maybe it is because you are not winning souls. Maybe it is because you fail to keep praying. But God promises that you can pray and receive answers from the Lord. ARE YOU GETTING YOUR PRAYERS ANSWERED?

CHAPTER FOUR

PRAYING IN THE HOLY GHOST

"But ye, beloved, building up yourselves on your most holy faith, praying in the Holy Ghost." (Jude 20)
Anything that you and I do in the Holy Ghost we do under His influence and supervision, as well as in His power. Get the statement I am about to make. What the Holy Spirit supervises He empowers. What He does not supervise He does not empower. That means that if I am to have power in my preaching He has to supervise my preaching. If I am to have His power in my soulwinning He has to supervise my soulwinning. If I am to have power in my prayer closet He must supervise my prayer life.

There are several things you and I need to understand about the Holy Spirit. First of all He is not a seducing Spirit. We have a crowd of folks who say, "Well, this strange feeling came over me and I flipped over on the floor." It may have been a spirit, but it was not the Holy Spirit. That is not the way He operates. He will only control what I yield to Him. He will control exactly what I yield, not one bit more. Here is the key phrase to everything I want you to understand. I am as yielded to the Holy Spirit of God as I am obedient to the Scriptures that He breathed.

You say, "Oh, Holy Spirit, fill me," while you are living in disobedience. You are praying a vain prayer. You can pray four hours a day for the fullness of the Holy Spirit while you disobey the Word of God and you will have no power with God.

Romans chapter eight is the Holy Spirit chapter of the Bible. He is mentioned nineteen times. God often dedicates an entire chapter to a certain topic in the Scriptures; a major personality, a member of the Godhead, or a doctrine. If I am going to pray under the influence and supervision of the Holy Spirit I had better find out what He wants me to do and what His ministry is. Four of the nineteen verses in which He is mentioned have to do with His ministry in our prayer lives.

In Romans 8:15 the Bible says, *"For ye have not received the spirit of bondage again to fear; but ye have received the Spirit of adoption, whereby we cry, Abba, Father."* That word "Abba" is a term of endearment. By the work of the Holy Spirit of God I can come to my heavenly Father and use a word of endearment. I am His son by regeneration. I am born of the water and of the Spirit of God. The Holy Spirit gives me a supernatural birth into the family of God. But the Bible calls Him here the Spirit of adoption. That means I am a son of God two ways. Both ways the Spirit of God supplies the means. He is the one Who regenerates me in a supernatural birth and He is the one Who adopts me or places me.

You say, "What is the big deal? If I am a son one way, what does it matter?" Who was Paul writing to here? What Book is this? Romans. Did you know that according to Roman law a natural son could be disinherited? But an adopted son could never be disinherited. God wanted these people to understand that when they got saved the Holy Spirit made it so that they had the endearment of a natural son, and the security of an adopted son. Sounds like a pretty good deal to me.

Because of that I have access. Before I was saved I had no access to God. I could not come to Him and say, "Heavenly Father." It was not true. It is the work of the Holy Spirit that gives me access to start with. I dare say a lot of folks never get their prayers answered because they have never been born again. They have no access.

I am not obligated to every child in the neighborhood. If all the children in the neighborhood come to me I may do something for them, and I may have compassion, but I do not have the same obligation to everybody in the neighborhood as I have to those who call me "dad." I have a special obligation to those who call me "dad." God has a special obligation to those who honestly come and say, "Heavenly Father," because of the regenerating and adopting work of the Holy Spirit of God.

There is a second thing I want you to notice. In verse twenty-three the Bible says, *"And not only they, but ourselves also, which have the firstfruits of the Spirit, even we ourselves groan within ourselves, waiting for the adoption, to wit, the redemption of our body."* He did not say, "Even we ourselves jump the pew backs." "Even we ourselves run and shout." "Even we ourselves overflow with exciting emotion." You say, "Are you against all that?" No, I am not against folks getting excited, I just want you to know what the firstfruit of the Spirit is. If that were the firstfruit of the Spirit then the charismatics got it right.

Paul said, *"Even we ourselves groan within ourselves."* The Bible says under the influence of the Holy Spirit I learn to groan. It is natural for me to groan over my own needs. It is supernatural for me to groan over the needs of others. If the Spirit of God enables me to groan, He will help me to groan over those things God groans over. I am afraid that most of us in our groanings are not too concerned about the will of God, we are not too concerned about the heart of God, we groan about the things that we personally are concerned about. But if I am under the influence and supervision of the Holy Spirit He will enable me to groan for spiritual things. He will enable me to groan over sinners going to hell. That is not natural.

By the way, our values are not real deep. That is why you have to get a picture of a little bloated-bellied boy with broomstick arms and legs to get somebody to support missions. We do not care that they are going to hell. All we care about is their flesh. Poverty moves us but hell does not. That is how carnal we are. The Bible says the Holy Spirit of God supplies me with the proper burden. He enables me to groan. If I do not know how to groan it is because I am not praying under the influence and supervision of the Holy Ghost of God.

In Exodus 6:5 God says, "I have heard the prayers of my people." Is that what He said? He said, "I have heard the groanings of my people." Groaning got the attention of God. If God enables me to groan, and my groan is His groan, I already have His attention. Without the influence and supervision of the Holy Spirit you do not even have a proper burden. Your burden and what you will pray for is not anywhere near what God is burdened about, unless you are praying in the Holy Ghost of God.

Groaning is both an emotion and an exertion of energy. It boils down to fervency. The average person has never had a bead of sweat come down their face in the prayer closet. Most folks do not shed a tear in the prayer closet. They know nothing about wrestling and straining in the prayer closet.

The charismatic crowd has hyped flesh and they blame that on the Holy Spirit. I am for excitement. I think you ought to get excited about something. If you can get excited at a ballgame, you ought to get ten times more excited about preaching. I think folks ought to have some spirit and zeal and fervor about them. But the truth is, you can have all of that and not have any power in the prayer closet unless you allow God to produce a burden, a groaning in your soul over the things that He is burdened about. Real fervency is not worked up in the flesh. Real fervency is the moving of the Holy Spirit of God on a surrendered human spirit.

The reason we do not have fervency in most cases is the fact that we are not surrendered to the Holy Spirit of God. But under His leadership I groan. He enables me to have a proper burden and to groan for what He groans for.

Notice verse twenty-six. *"Likewise the Spirit also helpeth our infirmities."* This verse is speaking of our prayer lives. The Spirit makes our prayers effectual and powerful. You are not heard for your much speaking. You are not heard for your positive thinking. You are not heard because you will something to come to pass real hard.

I have heard people say, "What you have to do is have strong enough faith. If you will it to happen hard enough it will come to pass." You did not get that out of the Bible.

The word 'infirmity' means 'want of strength.' More strictly in our text it means 'the inability to produce results.' So the Holy Spirit helps my inability to produce results. I cannot produce a single result without Him. You do not influence God at all. You say, "How do you get prayers answered?" First of all the Holy Spirit has to influence you so that you pray right. Then you pray what the Holy Spirit tells you to pray and the Holy Spirit influences the Father.

Some of you gals get up and iron your husband's shirt. Suppose you got out of bed, got the shirt out, laid it on the ironing board, got the iron out and put that iron on every inch of that shirt. One problem. You took as long a time as it takes to iron a shirt. You covered every inch. You used the right instrument. You went through the right motions, but you did not plug the iron in. When you got finished the shirt was as wrinkled as it was when you started. There is no end result of the ironing because you were not plugged into the power source. Your ironing is not effectual. You need electricity to help your infirmity, your inability to produce results.

Suppose somebody comes into your house with a vacuum cleaner. They push it over every inch of the floor. They go under every chair. There is just one problem. They failed to plug the vacuum cleaner in. They can work up a sweat. They can go through the effort. They are using the right instrument. They are going through the right motions. They take the right amount of time. They cover every inch of the territory. But when they finish the floor is as dirty as when they began. Why? Because they have this infirmity. Without being plugged into the power source all of their effort has no ability to produce results.

Suppose somebody got a lawn mower and they began to push it all over your lawn. You cover every inch. It takes hours and hours. You work hard. You only forgot one thing; to start the lawn mower. You used the right instrument. You went through the right motions. You took the right amount of time. You worked up a sweat, but when you finished the grass was as high as when you started. You have this infirmity. The inability to produce results unless the power gets to the blade. You can push that mower around all day long and have no fruit.

We have a lot of people going through the right motions, using the right instrument of prayer, taking the right amount of time and covering all the relevant territory, but they have no end result to their prayers because they never get plugged into the power source. They are praying with an infirmity that has not been cured by the Spirit of God. It is the Holy Ghost of God that helps our infirmity, makes our prayers effectual and powerful before the throne of God and produces the answer.

The next statement says, *"For we know not what to pray for as we ought."* The Bible tells us what to pray for. But we do not know how to pray as we ought. We do not know how to ask God to give the answer. I may know what the problem is but I do not know exactly how the solution should come. And unless I am submitted to the Holy Spirit of God I do not know what the right solution is. I see the problem. I know the Scripture says it should be this way, but it is this way instead. I say, "We have a problem." I can do as the children of Israel did when Samuel's sons went bad. They said, "We want a king like all the other nations." They had a legitimate problem, they just did not let the Holy Spirit give them a solution. They brought heartache and disaster because they had their own solution.

I am afraid in many cases we are trying to tell God how to solve the problems instead of letting God tell us how to pray. In Luke 11:1 the Bible says that the disciples came to Jesus and said, "Lord, teach us to preach." That is not what it says? Well, who was the greatest Preacher that ever lived? It was Jesus. It is amazing that the disciples, who knew Him best, came to the greatest Preacher who ever lived and said, *"Lord, teach us to pray."* His disciples were more impressed with His prayer life than they were with His preaching. He did not just have an impressive delivery, He had the power of God and He was used. He had power in prayer.

He is not here any more to teach us, is He? Not in a physical body, not for Him to stand up and let us sit at His feet. But He did not leave us without a Teacher. In John 14:26 Jesus told the disciples, *"But the Comforter, which is the Holy Ghost, whom the Father will send in my name, he shall teach you all things."* Do you reckon that might include how to pray?

I found out a long time ago that the Holy Spirit of God is not going to try to teach me anything I do not want to know. I stopped trying to teach people who do not want to know anything. If they think they already know it, I am not going to bother trying to teach them. It will bounce off their hard head. The Spirit of God is not going to waste time trying to teach you how to pray when you think you already know and when you are not interested enough to ask Him.

Every time I get on my face if I am going to have the leadership of the Holy Spirit I need to ask Him to help me pray as I ought, to give me leadership since He is the Teacher. I am afraid that if I am not in submission to the Teacher my prayers are little more than vain repetition.

Notice something else in Romans 8:26. *"The Spirit itself maketh intercession for us with groanings which cannot be uttered."* It started out saying the Spirit maketh intercession with groanings, not tongues. It is not talking about what He makes me do. It is talking about what He does for me. It is not talking about what He tells me, it is talking about what He tells the Father.

The first thing the Holy Spirit did was teach me to groan. But thank God now He is groaning for me. He taught me how to groan for others. Now I have run the course. I have come to the end of my resources. The burden is so great I do not even know how to form into words what is on my heart. The Holy Spirit does. When I have no idea how to express myself to God if I will submit to the Holy Spirit I can be sure that He will express it for me. He will groan for me. If you have not been there you will be. So get a hold of what I am saying.

If you have not been to the place where the burden is so heavy and your heart is broken you do not even know how to ask God for what needs to be done, just hang on. You will be there. You had better learn this lesson well before you get there. Do not try to figure it out once you are there.

He prays for what I overlook, too. He prays for what I do not know how to communicate to God. We have two perfect Intercessors. It talks in Romans eight about the Holy Spirit who intercedes for me. Do you know what He is doing? When I run out of words and I do not know how to express myself, when the burden is too heavy for me to form words and my heart is broken, He goes to the Father for me and says, "This is what his heart yearns for. This will mend his heart. This is just what he needs."

But in verse thirty-four the Bible says I have another Intercessor. It says, *"Who is he that condemneth? It is Christ that died, yea rather, that is risen again, who is even at the right hand of God, who also maketh intercession for us."* You say, "He is doing the same thing." No, He is keeping me saved. The Holy Spirit is communicating what I do not have words to communicate, and the Lord Jesus, every time I sin, every time I fail, intercedes. That is why I am saved eternally because He ever liveth to make intercession for me.

If He ever stopped interceding for you, you would not be saved. That is one of the reasons He had to be resurrected. Certainly He had to apply the blood, but He has to be alive today to intercede, as well.

In verse twenty-seven the Bible says, *"And he that searcheth the hearts knoweth what is the mind of the Spirit, because he maketh intercession for the saints according to the will of God."* It says in this verse that the Father knows my heart. If I am yielded and He places in my heart the right desire, then God can honor that desire.

The Spirit and the Father are one. When the Spirit groans, the Father groans. When He plants His groan in my heart God can answer. Some of the Holy Spirit's ministry is interference with my prayers. He interferes with my prayers to make God's answers better than my prayers. If I am praying in the Holy Ghost God's answers will always be better than my prayers because of the intercessory work of the Holy Ghost of God. He intercedes for me according to the will of God, not according to my carnal will.

So I pray and the Holy Spirit says, "Father, here is what he really means. He is just too dumb to tell you. That is not what he needs. He needs this." I pray and I ask God for something and the Holy Spirit says, "Here is what he really needs. Give him what he needs, not what he wants."

The story is told of a great preacher who was loved of his people. He was a godly man and rather elderly. He got very ill and his people were praying for his health. After several months he died and went to heaven. He went on to his reward. The people were very downcast and distraught. At the funeral service, a preacher who had been his friend for a lifetime came and preached. He said, "I suppose that some of you are in danger of assuming that God does not answer prayer. I would like to suggest to you that there were two conflicting prayers being prayed. You prayed and said, 'Oh, God, please leave him here because we need him so badly.' But the Holy Spirit's groan was, 'Father, please take him away, for they lean too heavily upon him and not heavily enough upon Thee.' The Holy Spirit of God got His prayer answered."

God's answers are better than our prayers. Without His access I have none. If I do not get His burden I do not have a proper burden. If I do not have His power I have none. If He is not in leadership I have no leadership. If I do not have His intercessory work for me, and His interference with my foolishness at times, I am in big trouble before God.

Every day, when I close my prayer time I say, "Holy Spirit of God, if I have prayed amiss, please correct that." I am sure that I pray amiss. I am sure that I ask for things in a wrong manner at times.

In James 4:2 the Bible says, *"Ye have not, because ye ask not."* He said the first problem we have is that we do not pray. The honest truth is, the average Baptist did not spend fifteen minutes in prayer this morning. Some of us have not spent fifteen minutes this week. There are only two reasons we do not ask.

If I needed ten thousand dollars I would not ask you. Do you know why? First of all I do not think you have ten thousand dollars. Secondly, if you have it I do not think you would give it to me. That is the same reason you do not pray. Either you think God does not have what you need or you think He would not give it to you. Which means you believe He lies. He made you the same promise He made to everybody else.

There is another problem. He said, *"Ye ask, and receive not, because ye ask amiss, that ye may consume it upon your lusts."* Let me ask you something. What has lusts? My spirit? or my flesh? My flesh. He did not say you pray for sinful things. He did not say you pray for wicked things. He did not say you pray for wrong things. He said you pray for the gratification of your flesh. I am supposed to pray for the glory of God, not for the gratification of my flesh. If the Holy Spirit is the One supervising my prayer life He wants to get the Father glory.

He said, "The problem is you have a carnal motive. You are driven by the flesh. The Holy Spirit has nothing to do with your prayer life. You are praying strictly according to your desire and fleshly will, and not energized by the Spirit of God."

Some of you have wrinkled clothes because you never get the iron out of the closet. Others of you have wrinkled clothes because you get the iron out and go through the right motions but never plug into the power source. Some of you have dirty carpet because you never get the vacuum cleaner out and use it. Others of you have dirty carpet because you get the vacuum cleaner out and push it around but you never plug into the power source. Some of you have high grass on your lawn because you never get the lawn mower out. Others of you have high grass because you get the lawn mower out and push it around but you never start it up.

Some of you do not get your prayers answered because you do not pray. Others of you do not have any prayers answered because you pray, but you are not praying in the Holy Ghost. You are praying in the flesh. I dare say if some of you do not learn to pray in the Holy Ghost you will not stay in church. You will not be able to. You are going to be carnal. You will not be able to get what you need to keep serving God. You will not even know what you need to keep you going.

Praying in the Holy Ghost is the only kind of praying that is going to change things. What is it today? You have not been praying? Or have you been praying in the flesh? I do not mean praying for wicked things. I mean praying in the energy of the flesh. I trust that today God has spoken to your heart if you have not been spending the time, the effort, the energy, or the hours in prayer.

We sing "Sweet Hour of Prayer" when, if the truth

be known, we would have to sing "Fleeting Moment Of Prayer." Most of us have never prayed an hour. Ask God to help you have an honest to goodness prayer life.

Some of you pray, but you have not been praying in the Holy Ghost, under His influence and supervision. By the grace of God, today, yield to His leadership in your prayer life. Learn to pray in the Holy Ghost.

CHAPTER FIVE

PRAYING ACCORDING TO THE WILL OF GOD
HOW TO GET ALL OF YOUR PRAYERS ANSWERED

"And this is the confidence that we have in him, that, if we ask anything according to his will, he heareth us: And if we know that he hear us, whatsoever we ask, we know that we have the petitions that we desired of him." (I John 5:14,15)
This passage sounds to me like a promise. It sounds to me like a sure thing. It sounds to me that if I can pray in such a way that God hears me then God is going to answer, if I pray according to the will of God. Nothing lies beyond the reach of prayer but that which lies beyond the will of God. In other words, anything that I ask of God I can get in prayer. Anything that is right and good and will glorify God and is according to His will can be obtained in prayer.

When God hears, I am going to have a one hundred percent success ratio in my prayers. The Bible says, *"...if...he hear us,...we know that we have the petitions that we desired of him."* You say, "Do you mean God does not hear us sometimes?" That is what the Scripture says. "You mean He does not know what you said?" No, that is not what 'hear' means. The word 'hear' in the Bible means 'to hear with the intent to do something about it.' Let me prove that to you. When it talks about us hearing it says, *"So then faith cometh by hearing, and hearing by the word of God." (Romans 10:17)* That does not mean that just because I heard a Bible verse I have more faith. When I hear the Bible with the intent to obey the Bible that will produce faith in my life.

God knows what everybody thinks as well as what they say. There is nothing that is not observable to God Almighty. The darkness is light to God. There are no secrets from God. Nothing is hidden from God. He knows everything that I even think about as well as what I do.

The Bible says that sometimes God does not hear with the intent to answer. If God hears me with the intent to answer, then I can know that I am going to have my request. If I will pray in the will of God, He will hear me with the intent to answer.

What does it mean to pray according to the will of God? First of all, the lost person is not in a position for God to hear him. There is proof of that in John 9:31. The Bible says, *"Now we know that God heareth not sinners."* That means that God does not hear the lost person who is outside of Jesus Christ with the intent to answer his prayer, unless it is a prayer of repentance and faith in Jesus Christ. If you have never been saved, if you have never been born again, you are not on praying ground. God is only going to hear a prayer of repentance and faith in Jesus Christ. If you will call upon the Lord Jesus and ask Him to save you, God will answer that prayer. Then you are in a position as a child of God, as a son of God, for Him to hear and honor your requests.

Before I can come to the Heavenly Father, I have to get into the family. Before I can come and ask my Father for anything, I have to be His son. I have to be in the family before I have any right to come to Him and expect an answer. When I get saved that puts me into that position.

The disobedient Christian does not have any authority in his prayers. In Psalm 66:18 the Bible says, *"If I regard iniquity in my heart, the Lord will not hear me."* When the psalmist said that, did he mean that God would not know what he said? No, God heard what he prayed. If I willfully keep something in my life, if I harbor something in my life that is iniquity, that is a willful violation of the law of God. When I regard iniquity in my heart and will not repent and will not part with it, I cannot get my prayers answered.

These are the three things that make my prayers powerful and make them so that God will hear. Praying according to the will of God means that I am to pray while I am in the will of God. *"The Lord...is...not willing that any should perish, but that all should come to repentance." (II Peter 3:9)* Until I get saved I am not in the will of God. *"If I regard iniquity in my heart..."*, if I know better but do not do better, *"the Lord will not hear me."*

It is one thing to be ignorant of the truth. It is another thing to know better and not do better. If I do not know any better it is still wrong, but it is not a willful violation. God is looking at my motive as a believer, and God will tolerate a mistake but He will not tolerate rebellion. I can make a mistake and get prayers answered, but I cannot go against the known will of God and get my prayers answered. I cannot live in known sin and rebellion and get my prayers answered. The first thing that has to do with getting my prayers answered is being in the will of God. I must be right with God, in tune with God, in the will of God, performing what God says I am supposed to perform. That puts me on praying ground. It puts me in a position that God will hear me. But when I am outside of the will of God I put a barrier up that keeps God from hearing me.

God did not put the barrier up. My disobedience becomes a barrier that makes the heavens brass. God knows what I am doing and He knows what I am saying, but He does not hear me with the intent to do what I am asking Him to do when I am out of the will of God and going my own way in spite of what I know the Scriptures teach.

If I know what the Bible says about something I must obey to be in the will of God. God commands me to be in church. He says not to forsake the assembling. So I am out of church but I am praying for all these things I want to get. I am not going to get anywhere. I am supposed to separate from the world. If I know something is wrong, but I am going to continue to do it, I am not going to get my prayers answered.

We have all kinds of people who know what the Bible teaches about separation and standards. They say, "I know, but..." They have somebody lost that they want to see saved. They say, "I do not know why I cannot get an answer." They may have some personal need they are asking God to meet and it is going unmet. God is interested in meeting my personal needs, but there are certain things that qualify me to come before God with some authority and expect an answer, and one of those things is praying while I am in the will of God.

If I am promiscuous in my lifestyle and doing things that God said I ought not to be doing, I can pray all I want but I am not on praying ground. I am not praying according to the will of God because I am not praying while I am personally abiding in the will of God.

In John 15, the great fruit bearing chapter, Jesus said, *"If ye abide in me, and my words abide in you, ye shall ask what ye will, and it shall be done unto you."*

The second thing is praying for the revealed will of God. I am supposed to pray for what God says is right. I am not just supposed to ask for what I want and disregard the will of God. I have a Bible. My Bible tells me what the will of God is.

People are always running around wondering what the will of God is. The truth is, the Bible tells us ninety-nine percent of what the will of God is. You only have to get about one percent anywhere else. Most of it is in print, in black and white. God gave me a Bible so that I would know the revealed will of God. I do not have to wonder what I should be praying for. I do not have to wonder how I should be living. I do not have to wonder what God wants me to do with my life. I need to pray in harmony with the Bible.

People pray for experiences that are not in harmony with the Bible. You may go ahead and pray for some tongues experience and get it, but God did not give it to you. You say, "I know my experience." I am not doubting your experience. I am just doubting that God gave it because it is not in harmony with the Bible. God is not going to answer a prayer that is not in harmony with the printed Word of God and not in harmony with the revealed will of God.

God is for getting people saved. So is it right for me to pray for people to be saved? Absolutely. I can pray with great confidence for sinners to be saved. Is it God's will for me to be a sacrificial giver? Yes, it is. Then would it be right for me to pray and ask God for money so I could give that money for the glory of God? Could I pray with some confidence and expectation? But if you are going to pray to be rich just so you can be rich, forget it. God never wants my motive to be riches for personal gain. It is all right for me to pray for finances so I can glorify God and be a blessing. It is all right for me to pray for finances so I can use them to take care of my family and do right. But for me to pray for wealth just so I can store it up and stash it away and have all this surplus while others do without, God is not going to honor that.

I must pray according to the Scriptures. The Bible says if I delight myself in the Lord He will give me the desires of my heart. When I am delighting in the Lord and in His law, He gives me my desires. That does not mean that if I think nice about the Lord and come to church every once in a while that He will give me every- thing I want and desire. It means if I delight in the Lord, God will give me right desires. God will give my heart the right desire and then God can honor my desires because He gave them to me.

We live in a society where people do not think they need to pray. The average Christian does not need to pray. He can work too many hours overtime and make too much money. He can do it all without God. If you would ever learn how to pray you might not have to miss church to work overtime. Everybody has an excuse and it is always logical, but if there be a God and He ordained a church, if He made His streets out of gold and His gates out of pearls two hundred and twelve feet high, and His walls made out of every kind of precious stone, I imagine He may be able to meet our needs if we put Him first and pray for His will. I think maybe God could take care of us a whole lot better than we can take care of ourselves out- side of the will of God.

The third thing is praying according to the specific leadership of the Holy Spirit. Ephesians 6:18 says, *"Praying always with all prayer and supplication in the Spirit."* To pray "in the Spirit" means to pray under His influence and under His supervision. Any- thing I do "in the Spirit" I do under His supervision. Instead of me trying to tell the Holy Spirit what to do, I let Him tell me what to do. In Romans 8:26 the Bible says, *"Likewise the Spirit also helpeth our infirmities: for we know not what we should pray for as we ought."* Paul said, "I have this infirmity. I do

not even know how to pray or what to pray, and even
when I know what is right according to the Bible, I am
not sure how to pray. I am not sure what to ask God to do
about this situation."

Sometimes I may need to ask the Holy Spirit of
God to give me leadership as to how this situation ought
to come to pass, how I should pray about this. What
should I ask God to do about it? Just how should I ask
God to meet the need?

The Bible tells us what to pray for. The Holy Spirit
helps us to pray as we ought, or to pray for what the Bible
says in the proper manner, asking for the proper things.
Even when I am aware of what to pray, I lack the
knowledge of how to ask God to meet the need.

Many of us pray like the little girl who asked her
dad for fifty cents. She was thirsty and wanted a drink.
Her father handed her a fifty dollar bill. She said, "No,
Daddy. I want fifty cents." He said, "Here, Honey. This
is a lot more than fifty cents." She said, "I want fifty
cents." She did not understand. He gave her a hundred
times what she asked for. She could have bought a hundred drinks with it, but she wanted fifty cents. I am
afraid that many times that is how we pray. God wants
to give us a hundred times what we ask for, but in some
cases our modesty in the prayer closet is an insult to God.
We are so modest about what we ask for, and we are so in
the dark about what we pray for, we do not think God
could give us more than what we pray for and we do not
think He would. We feel in our hearts that God is not
powerful enough to grant our big requests. We had better
ask modestly. He might run out of power.

The leadership of the Holy Spirit of God will help
me to come boldly to the throne of grace and find mercy
and grace to help in time of need. That is not necessarily
to help me, although I can get help for myself. God gives

me mercy and grace to help somebody else in their time of need too.

The same Holy Spirit who influences me to pray a certain way influences the Father to send the answer. Do not fall out of your seat when I say this. When you pray, you do not influence the Father. You do not influence God. God influences God. You are not in a position to influence God. That is why we have a mediator who is the God-man. Jesus, being one hundred percent man, can understand my infirmity. He can comprehend. Then, being one hundred percent God, He can go and communicate with God. If the Holy Spirit first influences me as to how I should pray and how He wants it done, then He will influence the Father to answer. The same Holy Spirit who tells me how to pray will influence the Father, because God can influence God.

The Holy Spirit of God is the one who is to lead me and guide me as to how I ought to pray. The Bible tells me what to pray, and the Holy Spirit tells me how I ought to pray. When the Holy Spirit directs my prayer life, then I am praying for His will, His way, and God will answer.

Most of the time we spend all of our effort trying to change God's mind instead of letting God tell us how we should pray and going His way.

Jesus is a perfect example of somebody praying according to the will of God. In John 11:41-42, when He came to the tomb of Lazarus, He lifted up His voice before all the people and prayed. *"Jesus lifted up his eyes, and said, Father, I thank thee that thou hast heard me. And I knew that thou hearest me always."* Why? Because Jesus always did the will of the Father. Jesus always prayed according to the will of God. Jesus always operated in the energy of the Holy Spirit while He was here.

Jesus said, "I know that You always hear Me."

That means if God always heard, then Jesus always got His prayers answered. John 8:29 says Jesus did always those things that please the Father. How often was He in the will of God? All the time. If He did always those things that please the Father, then He did never those things that displease the Father. Is that right? It does not say most of the time He did the right thing.

Not only did Jesus live in the will of God, but He prayed for the will of God. He prayed according to the Scriptures. In Matthew 26:39 He said, *"Father, if it be possible, let this cup pass from me: nevertheless not as I will, but as thou wilt."* He was saying, "There is a certain way I would like to see this turn out, but I am not going to try to impose My will above God's."

Jesus is God in flesh, but when He emptied Himself He operated as a Spirit-filled man. When He came to the Father He came with the same respect that I have to come with. He said, "I am not going to try to change Your will. This is what I would like, nevertheless what thou wilt." He said, "You go ahead and do it Your way."

The Bible says Jesus was led of the Spirit. He went forth in the power of the Spirit. He operated in the Spirit of God. The Father always heard and answered Him because He always prayed according to the will of God. He was always in the will of God when He prayed. He always prayed for the revealed will of God, and He always prayed according to the leadership of the Holy Spirit. He never deviated from that program. He always got His prayers answered.

I want to see people saved. God wants to see them saved worse than I want to see them saved. Do not get the idea that you are going to get God interested in soulwinning. Do not get the idea that you are going to get the Holy Spirit interested in going after sinners. He has already been going after sinners. He has been trying to get you involved. He has been trying to get you interested. He has been trying to get you dedicated. He has been dedicated from the foundation of the world. Nobody has to try to get Him involved in soulwinning. He is involved and trying to get you in.

It is God's will for people to be saved. The Bible says so. The Bible says, *"The Lord...is...not willing that any should perish, but that all should come to repentance."* God wants people to be saved. He does not want them to go to hell. If I am going to see this prayer come to fruition and see people saved, that means I need to be in the will of God myself.

The first thing I need to do is be a soulwinner. If I am going to pray and ask God to save somebody then I need to be a soulwinner. I need to be in the will of God as far as soulwinning. It is God's will for me to win souls. He said, *"Go ye into all the world, and preach the gospel to every creature."*

Is it right for me to pray for people to be saved? If I am going to pray for sinners to be saved I need to be in the will of God personally while I pray. That means I have to be a soulwinner myself while I am praying for sinners to be saved.

I can pray with confidence because the Bible gives examples of people like Paul praying for sinners. He said in Romans 10:1, *"...my heart's desire and prayer to God for Israel is, that they might be saved."* Not only am I supposed to be in the will of God as I pray, I am supposed to pray according to what the Bible says. If Paul prayed for sinners to be saved, and God recorded it in the Scriptures, it is right for me to pray for sinners to be saved. Now I am praying according to the Scriptures.

Then I go a step farther. As the Spirit of God gives me leadership, I can know whom I ought to pray for specifically and how to pray for them specifically. I can pray for those sinners' hearts to be tendered and that God will deal with them and they will be saved.

The same Holy Spirit who is convicting somebody's heart can tell me to pray for them. God can burden me for certain people. In the prayer closet I can pray for those people.

Is it God's will for me to be filled with the Holy Spirit? Yes. So it is right for me to pray for the fulness of the Spirit of God. It is right for me to ask Him to be in charge of my life and in control. If I am going to pray for the fulness of the Spirit of God I must be in the will of God. I must empty myself. I cannot ask the Holy Spirit to fill a full cup. I cannot ask Him to fill what is already full.

In the will of God, if I want the Holy Spirit's fulness, I have to empty myself of myself. I must die to self so the Spirit can take charge.

There are many Bible examples of people praying for the fulness of the Holy Spirit of God. I am commanded to ***"be not drunk with wine, wherein is excess; but be filled with the Spirit."*** I know that it is Scripturally right to pray for the fulness of the Spirit of God. Then I can ask the Holy Spirit to fill me and give me specific leadership and use that power that He puts in me to get a job done.

Is it God's will for His work to grow and His church to succeed? Yes. If I am going to pray that way, I need to be in the will of God helping the church to grow while I pray. We have too many pew riders and not enough laborers. We have too many spectators and not enough participants.

It is easy to criticize from the sidelines. Most people who are sports buffs have never played a down of football in their lives but they are experts. They will sit there and criticize.

I remember when I was playing football in high school. There was a guy sitting there in the stands who never played a minute of football. We had about twenty-six players on the team. I played offensive right tackle and defensive right tackle. I played on the kickoff team and on the receiving team and on the extra point team. I played every tick of the clock.

We played some big schools. We would get into the third or fourth quarter and I was bloody and dirty and tired and nearly dehydrated and exhausted. I would miss a block and some little old squirrel in the stands who never even touched a football would yell, "Hey, you big dummy!" What did he know about it? If you are going to sit there and criticize, come on down here. We will put you on the line and see what you can do.

Everybody thinks they know everything about building a church. It is easy when you are a spectator. But church building is not a spectator sport. Everybody is supposed to be a participant. If I am going to pray for the welfare and the growth and the success and the prosperity and the benefit of the church, I need to pray while I am in the will of God helping the church to grow and succeed.

In Acts chapter two and Acts chapter four they prayed for the church to succeed. That is what the apostle Paul did when he was praying for all the churches. In every epistle he was praying for their success.

God might burden my heart for a specific ministry of the church as the Holy Spirit gives me leadership. He will help me to pray. You had better watch that praying, though. It is liable to get you involved. That is why most of us do not want to pray.

Is it God's will for sin to be confounded and righteousness to be enthroned? You had better believe it is. God is a holy God. So if I am going to pray for God to bless the nation and straighten out all these crooked politicians, and I do not tithe, I am as crooked as the politicians. Some of you have a hard time with that, don't you?

In Romans chapter two Paul said, "Do you think you are going to pray for something while you are guilty of the same thing and then escape the judgment of God? You are a hypocrite." You are praying for it to be straightened out on one level, and it is wrong in your life. We are always praying for things to be made right and we are not doing right.

I have Bible illustrations and examples that show that it is right for us to pray for the things of God and righteousness to be enthroned and sin to be confounded. I have that command of God. I am supposed to pray that way. It is right for me to do. It is good for me to do. The first thing I have to do is be in the will of God myself. Then I have to be praying according to what the Word of God says. Then the Spirit of God must lead me in my prayers.

I preached a sermon called "The Weapon of Prayer." Prayer is a weapon God gave us to use to confound the devil. The Spirit of God may give me a burden to pray against a specific strong hold of the devil. I am supposed to pray against the devil. That is clear in the Bible. I am supposed to pray while I am not letting the devil influence me and I am right with God, doing what God said, praying in the will of God, praying for the will of God to be done.

While I am praying for God to get glory I may as well go ahead and glorify Him myself. *"Whether therefore ye eat, or drink, or whatsoever ye do, do all to the glory of God."* If I am going to pray for God to be glorified, the first thing I must do is be in the will of God while I am praying, and glorify God while I am praying.

I have a verse that tells me to pray for the will of God and to pray for God to be glorified. I am supposed to be glorifying God while I pray for God to be glorified, and I may pray for a specific way to glorify God. God wants us to be specific in our prayers, and the Holy Spirit is the one who gives us the specifics. If I am not careful, I will end up trying to tell God what to do instead of letting the Holy Spirit tell me what to pray for, and the Holy Spirit going back to the Father and saying, "This is what we need." God influences God. He is going to go ahead and take care of it. I can count on that prayer being answered.

It is pretty dangerous to pray outside of the will of God and not to be concerned about God's will. A preacher friend of mine told me a story. He said that there was a lady in his church who had a son. That son had been involved in a lot of sin and wickedness. His life was really in bad shape. Somehow he became very ill. He was taken to the hospital and had lapsed into a coma. He had a very high fever.

The doctors told his mother that he would not live through the night. He was not responding to their treatment. That lady was a saved lady, a member of the church. She turned to the preacher and the others from the church who were there at the hospital to try to help and comfort her. She said, "We are going to go into surgery with my son and we are going to pray for my son. If you are going to pray and say, 'If it be Thy will,' do not even come in. I do not want you to be in the room if you are going to say, 'If it be Thy will.' I do not care if it is God's will. I know what I want. I want my son to live and I want him raised up off of that bed."

A few people did not go in. Several did go in. They had about a thirty minute prayer meeting. The boy did a turn around.

You say, "In spite of the fact that she said she did not care if it was God's will?" The boy got out of the hospital, but his life was still a wreck. Two months later that same boy committed suicide.

The mother came to the funeral home and the man of God was there. She came up to the preacher and said, "I am sorry. I owe you an apology. I owe God an apology. I was wrong as I could be at the hospital. Now, I wish I had let him die at the hospital. I believe that was the will of God."

God's will is always better than your will. If she had prayed for God's will, her boy would have died of natural causes. She would not have gone through the misery of a suicide. You never know what is going to come out of a prayer when you are not interested in the will of God and all you are interested in is your own will. You may just hurt yourself.

God wants me to pray according to His will. He said, *"If we ask anything according to his will, we know that he heareth us: And if he hear us, we know that we have the petitions that we desired of him."* He said, "If we pray according to the will of God, we can be sure that the answer will come." If I pray while I am personally in the will of God, performing the will of God, if I pray for the revealed will of God Scripturally, and I pray under the influence and supervision of the Holy Spirit, I can be sure that all of those prayers will be answered. That excites me. It is a sure promise.

If there ever was a generation that needed some answers from God, we are living in it. I will guarantee you there is not an honest person alive who does not need to get a prayer answered today. You say, "How are you going to do it?" Nothing lies beyond the reach of prayer but that which lies beyond the will of God. Pray while you are in the will of God. Pray in accordance with the revealed will of God. Pray according to the specific leadership that the Holy Spirit gives you.

If I pray according to the will of God, according to those three things that we just looked at, I can be sure and have confidence that He will answer and meet the need.

CHAPTER SIX

WHY PRAYERS ARE NOT ANSWERED

"My God, my God, why hast thou forsaken me? why art thou so far from helping me, and from the words of my roaring? O my God, I cry in the daytime, but thou hearest not; and in the night season, and am not silent. But thou art holy, O thou that inhabitest the praises of Israel. Our fathers trusted in thee: they trusted, and thou didst deliver them. They cried unto thee, and were delivered: they trusted in thee, and were not confounded. But I am a worm, and no man; a reproach of men, and despised of the people." (Psalm 22:1-6)
Many of the Psalms have a three-fold meaning. They have a primary interpretation. They have a personal application. They also have a prophetic revelation. This is what is known as a Messianic Psalm, one that portrays the suffering of the Lord Jesus Christ in the New Testament. It is one I turn to very often when I am preaching on the cross.

David is speaking here prophetically, but he is also speaking of his heart's desire to get his prayers answered. Notice the first words, *"My God, my God, why hast thou forsaken me?"* These are the words that the Lord Jesus Christ spoke from the cross. That was no coincidence. This is a Messianic Psalm. The fifty-first Psalm and the thirty-eighth Psalm and others are Psalms of repentance. David was repenting of his sin with Bathsheba. When he did he began to see victory. He began to get prayers answered. He began to see God pour out His blessings once again, although he did pay the price for his sin. You never sin without paying for it.

David was forgiven by God when he repented, but he still reaped the results of his sin. He lost three sons over his sin with Bathsheba. He lost the son that was born of the adulterous affair. He lost his son Amnon after he had committed incest with Tamar. Absalom got angry at Amnon and killed him. Then Absalom got greedy and tried to take the kingdom from his father. Finally, Absalom was killed by Joab. David never again had a happy home. The sword and grief never did depart from his house.

In the twenty-second Psalm David was in a place where he was not getting any prayers answered. We are not going to look at the prophetic application about the Lord Jesus. The primary thing that is taught here is that David was in a drought, as far as getting prayers answered. The heavens were as brass. David could not seem to get through to God. He prayed and he wept, but he could not get an answer.

Nothing lies beyond the reach of prayer but that which lies beyond the will of God. God is a loving God who wants to give us things. He wants to save our loved ones. But we have to pay the price in prayer. There are different price tags on different people. You may not understand that, but they are owned by the devil. There is not the same amount of prayer and agony for every individual. Some people, after just a few times of prayer, will be gripped in their hearts by God. But some people are so bound up by sin, so captivated by Satan, that it takes much praying and much fasting and much labor in prayer.

Supplication is literally laboring in prayer. That is sweating in prayer, laboring and working in the prayer closet. Praying, and pleading, and begging with God, pouring our hearts out and taking hold of the throne of God. "I have to have it. I have to have it." Sometimes it takes that for a long time to see some people saved.

One thing that causes a problem to getting prayers answered is that unsaved people cannot get prayers answered. John 9:31 says, *"We know that God heareth not sinners."* The closest thing to an answer to prayer for an unsaved person that I can find in the whole Bible is in Acts chapter ten. Cornelius was a devout man. He feared God. He wanted to do right. He prayed to God with supplication. God sent an angel to tell Cornelius, "Go and find Peter and he will come and tell you how to get saved."

That is what God will do for a sincere person who really wants to please God. God will send by a soul-winner. I meet unsaved people many times who say, "This is unusual, but I was praying that someone would come by." I have had that happen to me a dozen times.

I walked to a door after praying for the Holy Spirit to guide us one night. There were some people gathered around the Bible in the front room. They looked startled. I said, "Hey, you are reading the Bible. Do you understand what you are reading?" They said, "No." I said, "I am a preacher. May I step in and show you how to go to heaven when you die?" They said, "Oh, that is wonderful. We were just saying how we wished someone could help us understand this thing about being saved."

An unsaved person is not God's child. You cannot get things from God if you are not His child. You cannot claim the promises of the Bible until after you have been born again, until after you become a child of God. Sometimes unsaved people will have a child or a loved one who is sick. I tell them, "The best thing you can do is to give your heart to the Lord Jesus Christ and get on your face in prayer before God. That is the only thing you can do to change it." Many times we are so selfish we are not willing to give our sin up and repent of it in order to be a help to someone else.

There is a second reason why prayers are not answered. It is because we just do not pray. That is what God said in James 4:2, *"Ye have not because ye ask not."* We are always going about trying to meet our needs. Do you know that it pleases God to meet our needs. If you are a father or a mother then you like for your children to be dependent on you. I like for my wife to depend on me. I like for her to have to lean on me. I like for my daughters to need me. I do not want them to try to make it on their own. I want them to come to me, to need my help. I desire that. I hunger for that. I enjoy that. I like to feel needed. So does God.

You would be surprised just how much God's desires are like our desires. God loves us and wants to be loved. God wants us to learn to depend on Him and ask Him for things. He wants to give His children things.

Getting an answer to prayer is not overpowering or overcoming God's unwillingness. It is laying hold of His willingness. God is willing and desirous to give us things. If there was ever a man of prayer it was John Rice. I remember Dr. Rice saying one time that he had a dream. He dreamed that he went to heaven and the Lord took him into a great storeroom. There were bricks of gold and new cars and clothing. There were all types of things. He said, "Lord, what is all this?" God said, "This is what you could have had, if you had just asked for it and claimed it." Dr. Rice said at that point he began to get more things from God than he ever had. More than ever, he realized that God has all kinds of things He wants to give to us, but we just have not been asking for them.

I have been asking for things right and left lately. And I have been getting them. I have been getting more prayers answered than I ever have. It is the most exciting thing to me.

I talked to an old atheist. I tried to win him to Christ. He said, "That Christianity stuff is just a myth. There is nothing real about it. It is just a crutch to lean on." I said, "If you really believe that, I want you to explain some things to me." He thought I was going to ask him about creation. He thought I was going to ask him about something scientific. I said, "I want you to explain to me how I have had seventy definite answers to prayer in the last ninety days." He started to say it was coincidence. But not seventy of them.

In the early days of our ministry I had prayed for four months for a little car to tow behind our motor home. One day I got into a car with a preacher and he started down the road. He said, "How do you like this car?" I said, "I like it. It is nice." I did not tell him I was praying for a car. I did not tell anybody but God. He said, "It handles pretty good, doesn't it?" I said, "Yeah, it is nice. It is pretty roomy for a small car." He said, "Boy, you could use one like this, couldn't you?" I said, "Yeah, I reckon I could." He said, "I was just talking to my wife last night and we feel like God wants us to give you this car if you will have it." I said, "Glory to God! If you believe that is what God wants you to do, sure, I will take it. I have been praying for four months for one."

I prayed for a secretary and got one too. I pray for what I need. I expect an answer and I get answers from God. I will tell you why some of us do without. We do without simply because we just do not pray. We do not expect God to answer so we never ask for anything. We spend all of our time striving and trying to make it on our own. That is why some of us cannot get to church regularly, because we are not trusting God. We are striving and laboring instead of saying, "Dear God, I cannot make it on my own. I have a need. Would You feed me? Would You clothe me? Would You take care of me?"

I am not promoting laziness, but I am promoting obedience. If obedience to God causes you a shortage of money, God will make it up. If doing the will of God brings a shortage into your life, God will fill that need if you will simply ask Him. No one ever starved to death for being obedient.

The problem is we just do not pray. We try to get things done in the flesh. We try to get things done by human wisdom. We try to get things done by earthly power and strength and it just will not work. Some of you folks complain about everything. You always talk about what you do not have and what you need. But I will guarantee that you never go before the throne of grace and spend half an hour pleading with God for what you complain about all day long. You deserve to do without. He said, *"Ye have not because ye ask not."* If people would pray as much as they complain, they would not have anything to complain about.

There is another reason why we do not get prayers answered. It is because of unconfessed sin in our lives. David's problem was not that he was not praying. He said, "The heavens are as brass." He was pleading with God. He was weeping. He was trying to get an answer but he could not. The Bible says in Psalm 66:18, David speaking again, *"If I regard iniquity in my heart, the Lord will not hear me."* That does not mean that He does not know what is going on. God knows what you think as well as what you say. What he is saying is that God will not honor my prayers until I cleanse the sin out of my life.

It says the same thing in Isaiah 59:1-2, *"The Lord's hand is not shortened, that it cannot save; neither his ear heavy, that it cannot hear: But your iniquities have separated between you and your God."* The things that you think are little, insignificant sins will keep you from getting answers from God.

If you and I loved sinners like we say we do, if we loved our families, then we would not let a little thing like a pet sin or a bad habit, a pack of cigarettes, or beer in the ice box, or unisex clothing, stand in our way. We would be willing to get rid of it for the glory of God, to get our prayers answered, and to see God bless. We would be willing to clean up our lives. The things that you think are unimportant, the things that you think are just not big sins - griping, complaining, jealousy, inconsistency, unfaithfulness, laziness, are dirty, wicked sins in the eyes of God. He spends about one fifth of the Book of Proverbs condemning laziness and slothfulness, talking about the sluggard.

Our sins and our iniquities build a barrier, a wall, that makes it impossible for God to bless us. It makes it impossible for God to honor our prayers until we cleanse that sin out of our lives. In the first chapter of Isaiah God thunders out against sin. In verse fifteen He talks about the prayer life of His people, the nation of Israel. He said, *"When ye spread forth your hands, I will hide mine eyes from you: yea, when ye make many prayers, I will not hear: your hands are full of blood."* The Bible says I am to be a watchman over the souls of men. If I am not a soulwinner I have bloody hands. You will not get many prayers answered until you are willing to get your hands clean from the blood and try to make some kind of an effort to win souls to Christ. People who are not soulwinners are not great prayer warriors either. People who are great prayer warriors are great soulwinners. Why? Because you have to keep your hands clean to get prayers answered. Everybody does not have the same amount of ability, but everybody can do something to get people saved.

We overlook soulwinning and say, "That is not my

strong suit. That is not my bag. I am not a good talker. That is not my talent. That is not my special ability. That is not my area." No, it is God's command and your duty. When you do not do your duty as a watchman it will keep you from getting your prayers answered.

In Isaiah 1:16 God says, *"Wash you, make you clean; put away the evil of your doings from before mine eyes; cease to do evil; Learn to do well."* God said, "I absolutely will not hear your prayers. I will not give you answers to prayer until you get the sin out of your lives and cleanse yourselves. Turn from your sin and do right."

Most Christians will get about eighty-five or ninety percent right with God, but they are not willing to put the whole thing on the altar. They are not willing to surrender and yield themselves completely. That is why they do not get their prayers answered. He gave His all for us. He does not want our leftovers. He wants the firstfruits. He wants our best. He wants us to give ourselves to Him, lock, stock, and barrel.

I John 1:8-9 says if we say that we have no sin the truth is not in is. That is what some of you have been saying all along. You say, "I have no sin. I do not need to come to the altar. I do not need to walk an aisle. I do not need to get right with God. I am already right with God. There is no sin in my life. I am already perfect. I am already mature. I cannot go any farther. I am as right with God as I can be." You have not said that verbally, but you have said it by remaining in your seat when you should have been at an altar. God spoke to you and you knew you should have walked the aisle. You knew there was something in your life that was not just exactly the way it should be. But still you did not come.

"If we confess our sins, he is faithful and just to forgive us our sins, and to cleanse us from all

unrighteousness." That verse excites me. There are some things I know are wrong. If I will just be honest with God and ask God to forgive me for what I know is wrong, God says He will cleanse me of the things I do not know are wrong *"...and cleanse us from all unrighteousness."* He will purge me of the things I do not even realize I have done.

Confession is not just telling God what you have done wrong. Confessing and forsaking go together. Confession simply means that I say the same thing about my sin as God says about it. Some of us do not say the same thing about sin that God says about it. God thunders out judgment against it. God says He hates sin. But we love our sin. We hang onto it and say it is not such a bad sin. It is just a little thing.

There is another reason we do not get prayers answered. By the way, God is not trying to make it hard to get our prayers answered, but there are a few elements that have to be cared for. One of them is the matter of believing God. Many times we pray, but we really do not expect an answer. Sometimes, in spite of our unbelief, God does answer. A good example of that is in Acts chapter twelve. They were praying. "Oh, God. Let Peter out of jail. Oh, God, let him out."

Peter got out of jail. He came over and knocked on the door and they said, "No, that is not Peter. That is his angel. It could not be Peter. He is in jail." That is real faith, isn't it? That is like most of us. "Oh, God. Save so-and-so. I know he will not get saved, but I will pray for him anyway." Someone else is going to have to pray for him. That skepticism will keep us from getting our prayers answered.

The Bible says, *"But Jesus did not many mighty works there because of their unbelief."* We can limit the Lord in our unbelief. He responds to our faith. He will meet our need after we trust Him to. Psalm 78:41 says, *"They turned back, and tempted God, and limited the holy one of Israel."* It is possible, by our unbelief and infidelity, to keep God from blessing us.

Hebrews 11:6 says, *"He that cometh to God must believe that he is, and that he is a rewarder of them that diligently seek him."* So if I want to get my prayers answered I have to believe that God is, and that He is a rewarder of them that seek Him. He wants to reward me, He wants to bless me. Mark 11:24 says that whatsoever we ask of Him, believing, we shall receive. He said, *"All things are possible to him that believeth."* He said, *"Is anything too hard for the Lord?"* There is nothing too hard for God. No job is too big for Him. No prayer is too big to be answered by God. If you knew what I was praying for you would know I believe that. I expect to get prayers answered. The Bible says, *"We walk by faith, not by sight."*

In James chapter one, He tells us some things about faith and about doubt. *"If any of you lack wisdom, let him ask of God, that giveth to all men liberally, and upbraideth not; and it shall be given him. But let him ask in faith, nothing wavering. For he that wavereth is like a wave of the sea driven with the wind and tossed. For let not that man think that he shall receive any thing of the Lord. A double-minded man is unstable in all his ways."* God said, "You can ask me for things. But do not ask Me if you do not believe you are going to get it. Do not waste your time giving out petitions that you do not expect Me to meet. If I answered it you would not give Me the glory anyway."

God does everything He does for His glory and for His cause. That is why He created. That is why He has a plan of redemption. That is why He has us grow in grace.

That is why He started the church. You go verse by verse through the Bible and you will find that everything He did was for His glory. Many people do not get prayers answered because they do not expect an answer. Their unbelief limits God and prevents God from blessing.

Do you remember the father who came to Jesus? Jesus said, "Do you believe?" He said, *"Lord, I believe. Help thou mine unbelief."* He said, "I want to believe. I want to believe with all my heart. I believe to the best of my ability. But I have doubts and fears. Help me to believe You." God honored his prayers. Why? He had a little bit of skepticism there but he had a desire to believe God. He was yielding himself to the best of his ability. God says we are to believe Him for things, and when we do we will start getting prayers answered. When we do we can pray and see revival taking place. We can pray and have our financial needs met. We can pray and God will heal bodies.

God is able to heal. You hear people say, "Well, the days of healing are over." You have an extra hole in your head. God did not quit healing. There never was the kind of healing that is going on with the charismatic movement today, where they hit people in the head and knock them out. You will not find any of that in the New Testament. But you will find in James chapter five an exhortation for us. He said, *"Is any sick among you? let him call for the elders of the church; and let them pray over him, anointing him in the name of the Lord."* That is Scriptural.

Do you know what happens? These people get some wild fire and they scare us away from the real fire of God. These people got off on a tangent on healing and they scared us away from healing. God is as able to heal today as He ever was. I do not believe it is always God's will to heal like they say it is. They say if you are not healed it is because of sin in your life. That is a bunch of baloney. Some of the most godly Christians I have ever known have had sickly lives. They prayed for healing. Paul prayed for it, by the way. He sought the Lord thrice. God said, *"My grace is sufficient for thee."*

God does not always give us everything we ask for. Sometimes folks serve God a whole lot better in sickness than they would in health. It is not necessarily chastisement. It is just something that makes them more effective for God. God knows that. They will have a great reward in heaven because they had a great affliction here.

There is another thing that prevents prayers from being answered. That is unholy requests, or requests for the wrong motives, requests for the wrong things. *"Ye ask and receive not because ye ask amiss, that ye may consume it upon your lusts."* I have heard it said, "Well, God will take care of all your needs, but He did not say anything about your wants." That is not necessarily true. In Psalm 37:4 He said, *"Delight thyself also in the Lord, and he shall give thee the desires of thine heart."* If I am delighting myself in the Lord, if the Lord is the object of my love, the center of my life, if my life is wrapped up in Him, then my desires will be His desires, and He will always be able to give me the desires of my heart. That promise is not for everyone who is saved. That promise is for those who literally delight themselves in God.

When I am delighting in the Lord I will want to see people saved and I will pray for people to be saved. Most of the things I pray for everyday are not for me. I pray for other people. I pray for the work of God. I pray for preachers. I pray for people who are sick. I am not bragging. I am just saying that most of our prayers ought to be for others. If we will wrap ourselves up in praying and pleading for others He will look out for us. The problem is that when we are looking out all the time for ourselves God cannot answer our prayers because our hearts are not right.

When God answers prayer it is for His glory and honor. Psalm 50:15 says, *"And call upon me in the day of trouble; I will deliver thee, and thou shalt glorify me."* That means if I pray for things that are right, God will bless and answer my prayers and He will be glorified. Do you know why you cannot get your loved ones saved? They have never seen anything supernatural about your life. They have never seen you pray for anything and get it. One of the most powerful instruments that the Christian has in his hands is prayer. Not only because you can pray and get things from God, but when others see you pray and get answers they can see that there is something real about your Christianity. There is no glory to the man who is praying, just glory to the God of heaven who answers prayer.

If I do not pray to consume things on my lusts, I can expect an answer from God. If my prayers are all, "Give me this. Give me that. Gimme. Gimme." God says I am praying selfishly so that I can consume it on my lusts. He will quit answering my prayers because my desires are not His desires. I John 5:14-15 gives us another prayer promise. *"And this is the confidence that we have in him, that, if we ask any thing according to his will, he heareth us: And if we know that he hear us, whatsoever we ask, we know that we have the petitions that we desired of him."* That means if I will pray in the will of God I am sure of an answer from God.

He did not say He might answer. He did not say we might have the petitions we desired of Him. He said I will get my prayers answered. The average Christian does not believe that. The average person reading this message did not pray five minutes today. If you really believed in prayer, why wouldn't you talk to God and ask Him for the things you need? Why wouldn't you pray, if you really believed that prayer would work.

There is another thing the Bible says will cause our prayers to go unanswered. That is a bitter or an unforgiving spirit. Nothing quenches the Spirit of God quicker than an unforgiving, hateful spirit among Christian people. In Mark 11:24-25, Jesus said, *"Therefore I say unto you, What things soever ye desire, when ye pray, believe that ye receive them, and ye shall have them. And when ye stand praying, forgive, if ye have aught against any: that your Father also which is in heaven may forgive you your trespasses. But if ye do not forgive, neither will your Father which is in heaven forgive your trespasses."*

Most of us hold grudges, don't we? Most of us have an unforgiving spirit. Notice what else He said in Hebrews 12:15, *"...lest any root of bitterness springing up trouble you, and thereby many be defiled."* Bitterness, hatred, strife, jealousy and hard feelings will quench the Spirit of God and keep you from getting your prayers answered. In Matthew 5:23 Jesus said, *"Therefore if thou bring thy gift to the altar, and there rememberest that thy brother hath aught against thee; Leave there thy gift before the altar, and go thy way; first be reconciled to thy brother, and then come and offer thy gift."* Jesus said if you have wronged someone, or if someone has wronged you, go and settle the bitter feelings. Get them out of the way. Make it right with God. By the way, you will not make it right with God until you get it right with them.

You can pray all you want to, but as long as you do not clear the air with them you still have not taken care of it God's way. When someone offends us we are to go to them. The Bible says in Galatians 6:1, *'Ye which are spiritual restore such an one in the spirit of meekness."* You go to him if you are spiritual and you make it right. You make the effort. If not, it is going to hinder your prayer life.

Did you notice Jesus did not say, "Do not give"? Some people use that as an excuse and say, "Well, I am not right so I will not give." You are supposed to give whether you are right or not. But God said, "Do not leave the other undone. Get right with Me then I will honor and bless your gift." In Ephesians chapter four the Bible says we are supposed to learn to get along with one another. *'Let all bitterness, and wrath, and anger, and clamour, and evil speaking be put away from you with all malice: And be ye kind one to another, tenderhearted, forgiving one another, even as God for Christ's sake hath forgiven you."*

In the Book of Luke Jesus told of one man who had a big debt. He came in and told his master, "I do not know what to do. I cannot pay the debt. It is too big." The master said, "I will forgive you the debt." Let's say it was ten thousand dollars. That man went back out and saw someone who owed him ten dollars. He had just been forgiven a ten thousand dollar debt. He said, "Pay me." The man said, "Give me time. Be patient with me." He said, "No." He had him put into prison.

The Bible says the man that forgave him the ten thousand dollar debt got angry. He came back and said, "You mean I forgave you all of that, and you will not forgive that one little thing?" Friend, before you start holding a grudge remember what Jesus forgave you for. You had better stop and look at the pit from which you were digged. You had better look at the mire from which you came and realize God has forgiven you a billion dollar debt.

When someone does you wrong, you had better learn to forgive that little ten dollar debt. You are going to make God angry. God will not only not answer your prayers, He is liable to spank you as His child to try to get your heart tender and right.

When you look at the Bible you will never find Jesus fighting with anybody. They threw stones at Him, they cursed Him, they called Him everything in the book. They called Him an illegitimate child. This was God. He did not let that rattle Him. He still loved them. On the cross He said, *"Father, forgive them, for they know not what they do."* Stephen, when he was being stoned to death, said, *"Lord, lay not this sin to their charge."* Where is that kind of Christian today? Where is that crowd who says, "God, be merciful to them, in spite of their sin." We do not see much of that anymore. We are too worldly. We are too wrapped up in ourselves. Our little egos get hurt, and we cannot get over it.

Bitter feelings and grudges are poisoning your prayer life and your heart. They are ruining your own spirituality and that of those around you. They are keeping you from getting your prayers answered.

The devil will fight you the hardest when you are close to a great victory. So when you are ready to give up in prayer, hang on some more, because you are getting close to victory. When you just think you may as well quit, then pray some more. The answer is near, and the devil is fighting as he always does.

We will not have revival without praying people and without answers to those prayers. You are not going to see your loved ones saved unless you learn to pray. Many of us have not been praying like we should. Others have been praying, but there are obstacles standing in the way that keep us from getting our prayers answered.

God wants to answer our prayers. Do you want answers to prayer? Do you believe God? You need to remove the obstacles and get serious about the business of effectual, fervent prayer.

CHAPTER SEVEN

PRAYERS WITH FEET

This message comes from a very familiar passage, but I do not think the message is a very familiar thought. In Matthew 7:7, the Bible says, *"Ask, and it shall be given you; seek, and ye shall find; knock, and it shall be opened unto you: For every one that asketh receiveth; and he that seeketh findeth; and to him that knocketh it shall be opened."*

The Bible says, "Ask, and it shall be given you; ask, and ye shall find." Right? Is that what it says? Oh, that is not what it says? "Ask, and it shall be opened unto you." Is that what it says? That is not what it means, either. *"Ask, and ye shall receive; seek, and ye shall find; knock, and it shall be opened unto you."* Now, if God had meant the same thing all three times he would have used the same word all three times.

God wants us to learn something. Dr. Rice popularized this statement: "Prayer is asking and receiving." I have no qualms with that statement. Prayer is definitely asking. But you and I have a tendency to want to claim all three prongs of the promise without practicing all three prongs of the command. God said that I am supposed to ask and I will receive. I am supposed to seek and I will find. I am supposed to knock and the doors will be opened. You say, "What does that mean?" That means that there are some things that require a supernatural answer from God Almighty Himself. And the only thing that I can do is ask and keep on asking and keep on asking and keep on asking. There is no human instrument involved in the answer. It is going to be a direct answer from God.

Suppose I am burdened for someone who is ter-
minally ill, and he is in the hospital, and the doctors say,
"There is nothing more we can do for him. We have given
up. This is it. This is the end of our ability to help. He
is just not going to make it. He is a hopeless case." Now,
the only thing I can do about that is come to God and ask
and keep on asking and keep on asking. God can answer
and intervene supernaturally and heal that body.

If we are having some kind of an outdoor meeting
and bad weather is called for there is only one thing I can
do. I cannot do anything to change the weather except
ask and keep on asking and keep on asking the God who
controls the weather. God is able to meet the need. God
can supernaturally intervene.

However, all answers to prayer are not answers
where God does it Himself without a human instrument.
All answers to prayer are supernatural. All answers to
prayer are the result of God doing something. The honest
truth is there are some things that are not going to
happen without a human instrument. He said, *"Seek,
and ye shall find."* You say, "What do you mean, 'seek'?"
I mean you can go to the prayer closet and you can pray
tonight for people to be saved. But I have news for you.
God is not going to go soulwinning for you because you
prayed. God will go soulwinning with you. If you are
going to get that kind of answer, you are going to have to
ask, and seek, not just ask and then go back into the
other room and sit down. God is not going to do your
soulwinning for you. But if you will pray and ask God for
His power, and His presence, He will go soulwinning with
you. You must ask and seek to get that kind of an answer
to prayer. What you are doing is asking God to do something and making yourself available, asking God to use
you to accomplish that task.

There is a third thing. That is knock. There are

some things that you can ask for and seek. You ask God to meet the need. Then you put your resources to work, and it still comes up short. You are going to have to let other folks know what the need is and let God work in their hearts. Suppose I needed ten thousand dollars. I do not. I need twenty thousand. But suppose I needed ten thousand dollars. I come to God and I say, "Dear God, I need ten thousand dollars". It is right to pray for that. It is fine to ask God for that. While I am praying, I need to get into my billfold and get my hundred dollars out and put it in the plate. Now I am asking and seeking. My hundred is not what I need. I need ten thousand. I ask and I keep on asking and then I seek and use my resources, then I knock and appeal to somebody that maybe can meet the need. I let them know and let God work in their heart.

We have become impractical. Most of us are practicing Eastern mysticism instead of Bible Christianity. You think if you just will it to happen, if you think on it hard enough, it is going to come to pass.

But God is a very practical God and Christianity is a very practical religion. So God said to ask and keep on asking. And then seek and keep on asking. And knock and keep on asking. I never stop asking to seek and knock. But I knock while I continue to appeal to God, while I continue to bombard heaven with the request. I reach into my billfold and get my money out while I appeal to others who can meet the need. That is knocking. That is going beyond my resources. When I seek, I am using my resources. When I knock, I am coming to you for your resources. I first come to God and ask Him to meet my need. I make my resources available. When that comes up short, I appeal to others and let God work in their lives.

You never stop asking to seek and you never stop

asking to knock, but while you are asking you seek and you knock. That is Bible praying. If I will apply those principles God said that I can be assured of the answer.

This word 'ask' is a durative or linear verb. It means ask and keep on asking and keep on asking and keep on asking. You say, "How long do you ask?" Well, just keep it up till you get to heaven. You never quit asking to do anything, but while you ask, you seek and you knock in order to see these things come to pass.

Someone well said that prayer is not an excuse for being lazy and sorry. Prayer is not an excuse for you and me to be idle. A lot of people say they pray about something and the truth is that they breathed two words of prayer and went back to bed. Then they expect God to show up on the scene and do what He already commanded them to do. God's part, I cannot do. My part, He will not do.

I have never prayed and had money fall out of the sky. How about you? I never have prayed and had money pop out of the ground. I never have prayed and had the pages of my Bible turn into dollar bills. It has not happened. I have had lots of financial answers to prayer but God has always used a human instrument to answer those prayers. Sometimes I did not even know who the human instrument was, but God always used a human instrument to answer that prayer. God does use people. Do not lose sight of that.

You see, what we need are shoe-leather prayers. We need prayers with feet - our feet. My feet attached to my prayers and your feet attached to your prayers, that is what we have to have. Someone said, "Pray for a good harvest, but keep on hoeing." Imagine an old farmer going to the barn. He gets on his knees beside the tractor and says, "O, God. Give me the greatest harvest I have ever had. O, God. Give us a great harvest, a great increase." He gets down beside his tractor and prays, and then does not even start the tractor. He does not plow the field. He does not plant the seed. Do you think he is going to get his prayer answered? You say, "That guy is a nut." He is no nuttier than some of you. You do the exact same thing with your Christianity he would be doing with his farm. You pray and say, "O, God, give us souls. O, God, meet the need". Then you do not seek and you do not knock. You are impractical about your Christianity.

God wants me to pray and He wants me to learn to depend on Him but He does not want me to become a welfare case. Amen! God wants me to understand that there are certain responsibilities even within the confines of my prayer life, things I pray about, that I do not just pray about and then forget. There are some things that God is going to use me to accomplish and some things He is going to use other people to accomplish. I need prayers with feet - my feet. You need prayers with feet - your feet.

I have noticed that God's people are willing to pray for a lot bigger things than they are willing to work for. We pray great big prayers and then live little Christian lives. We pray for God to do big things and then we make small contributions instead of great sacrifices. We pray for lots of people to get saved and then do a little bit of soulwinning. Your prayer life needs to be consistent with your living. We need prayers with feet. We pray fervently and ask God sincerely for all the right things and then we cut the feet off our prayers and wonder why they do not come to pass.

If you only practice one-third of what Matthew chapter seven is talking about then you can only claim one-third of the answers. It is kind of like the little boy who went and stayed at his grandpa's house. He had not seen him for a long time. Grandpa was a very godly man. The little boy came and spent the night. The old man had family devotions with him before he went to bed that night. He read his Bible as he always did. Before he went to bed, the old man got down on his knees. He lived right down the block from a bar. Every conceivable kind of wickedness was practiced there. There had been murders there, rapes there, and every kind of filth. The old man was burdened about it. He prayed, "God, please. Somehow, burn that place down. Blow it down. Get rid of it."

Well, as the little fellow got down to pray, he followed suit. He prayed, "Lord Jesus. You know that is an awful place down there. I pray You would burn it down." They went on to bed that night. The next morning, Grandpa got up early and let the little fellow sleep. He got in his car and drove down the road. He looked over and there was nothing there but a pile of smoldering ashes. The place had burned to the ground. He quickly turned into the parking lot, made a U-turn, and headed back to the house. He was so thrilled. He woke his grandson up. He said, "Sonny! Sonny! Wake up!" He woke up and he said, "What is it, Grandpa?"

He said,"Sonny. Do you remember that place that we prayed about last night?"

He said, "Yes."

"Boy," he said. "For years I have been praying that God would burn that place down. Last night, for the first time, you prayed. I just went by and it is burned to the ground. Sonny, you must really have power in your prayers".

The little boy just shrugged his shoulders and said, "Oh, no, Grandpa. I just put feet to my prayers".

I am not suggesting that you go out and burn any buildings down. But I am suggesting that you get a whole lot more practical about your prayer life and that you recognize there are some things that God wants to use you to accomplish. That is why he burdened you to pray about it.

We pray for God to meet the needs of the church, then when there is an opportunity to be a blessing we are unavailable. "Oh, God, bless the church. Oh, God, You know we need a Sunday School teacher for the junior department. Oh, God, I pray You would raise up a junior department Sunday School teacher for those boys, but not me, Lord. Not me." Well, you sure are free with somebody else's life. You sure are free with somebody else's time.

We come to the prayer closet and we pray, "Oh, God, I pray that you would raise up somebody to run that Sunday School bus. You know those boys and girls need Jesus. They need to be saved. Somebody needs to pick them up. I pray that You would raise up a bus driver and a bus worker, but not me, Lord. Not me. Get somebody else. I will do the praying, Lord. Let somebody else work." Oh, no. You are supposed to pray and work, too. Your ministry is not praying without working. Everybody's ministry is to pray and to work.

The truth is, nobody is praying much these days. If we knew how much prayer goes on in the average church on any given day, it would scare us all to death. We need to pray practically and put feet to our prayers. What we do is pray for the right thing and then cut the feet off our prayers. We pray for a bus worker, but we are not going to do it. We pray for God to help out and get somebody to clean the bathrooms so that the preacher will not have to do it, but we are not going to do it. We pray for Sunday School teachers but we are not going to do it. We have no intention of God using us to be a Sunday School teacher. But we say we are burdened about that. Oh, really? You might need some prayers with feet. We pray for God to save sinners, then never go soulwinning. We never knock on a door. We never hand out a Gospel tract. We never witness on the job. We never learn how to win a soul.

Instead of finding a way, we find an excuse. We say, "Oh, God. Save sinners". Thursday night rolls around, or Saturday morning rolls around, and we do not go soulwinning. By the way, soulwinning is valid any day. You cannot go on the wrong day. You cannot go at the wrong time. You cannot go too often. The Bible says, ***"Daily in the temple, and in every house, they ceased not to teach and preach Jesus Christ."*** That is Book of Acts Christianity. Is that the kind you and I have?

We pray for sinners to be saved but we do not learn how to win a soul because if we do, we would not have an excuse. Boy, if we went to a soulwinning class and they gave us some methods, or we got a soulwinning tool that enabled us to do it, then we would not have an excuse. Better not do that. What will I use for an excuse then? What I want to know is, what are you going to use for an excuse at the judgment seat of Christ?

By the way, I am supposed to pray about people getting saved. In Luke 24:49, Jesus told the disciples, ***"Tarry ye in...Jerusalem."*** How long? Until you be endued with power. Then what? ***"Ye shall receive power, after that the Holy Ghost is come upon you, and ye shall be witnesses unto me, both in Jerusalem, and in all Judaea, and in Samaria, and unto the uttermost part of the earth."*** They prayed for ten days and the power of God fell. If they had stayed in that room after the power of God fell, if they had not gone out into the streets, if they had not witnessed, if they had not carried the Gospel outside the doors of that prayer meeting after the power of God fell, how many people would have been saved on the day of Pentecost? None! But that is the way you and I do it. We are going to pray them in.

There is nothing wrong with praying, but do not expect God to do the door knocking for you. You are going to have to ask and seek to claim an answer to those prayers for souls. We pray and then do not go and put feet to our prayers, yet we wonder why sinners are not being saved.

A true story is told of a collision between an excursion liner and a big steam ship about a hundred years ago on the River Thames. It was a dark, stormy night. When the collision took place, the loss of life was great. Over six hundred people went down in those dark, stormy waters. At the time of the accident, there were two men mooring their boats for the day. They had been out on the river all day working. Both of them had put in a long day. Both were tired and weary. Both heard the collision and the screams and cries of the people. One of those men said, "I am tired. I have had a long day. I am just too tired to go and help. I know what has happened. But surely, somebody will go and help. I am just too weary to do it myself. Besides, no one will see me slip off into this dense fog." So he did, and he went home. As he went off through the fog, I am sure he breathed a prayer, asking God to send somebody to salvage those lives while he went idly home.

The second man, when he heard the screams and cries, loosed from harbor and pulled for the wreckage with all his might. When he arrived, he loaded every woman and every child onto the boat until he could not load another on. Then he pulled away with a broken heart because there were literally hundreds perishing in the waters. Several weeks later, there was a coroner's inquest. Both of those men were called, even the man who thought he would not be found out when he slipped off into the dense fog.

One of these days you and I are going to be called to the judgment seat of Jesus Christ. We will look into the blazing eyes of fire of the Son of God Who died for sinners and commanded us to go and tell them. There will be no secrets there, and there will be no excuses there.

The first man was called into the presence of the coroner. He looked him in the eye. He said, "Did you hear the cries of those people?" As he dropped his head, he said, "Yes, sir. I did." The coroner said, "Are you an Englishman?" Once again he dropped his head and said, "Yes, sir, I am." The coroner asked a third question. He said, "Aren't you ashamed of yourself?" With tears streaming down from his eyes, the man said, "Yes, sir. The shame will never leave men until I die."

You mark my words, friend. You can go ahead and ask God to save sinners and not go out and knock on a door and not hand out a Gospel tract and not go soul-winning and not witness, but one of these days, you are going to the same inquest that I am going to. You are going to have to look into the face of Jesus Christ and give account. I do not want to hang my head and say, "I am ashamed." None of us are what we ought to be. But we do not have to be idle, doing nothing.

The first man prayed as he rowed off into the fog, but then he cut the feet off of his prayers.

The coroner asked the second man about his experience. He said, "Sir, did you hear the cries?" He said, "Yes, sir. I did." "What did you do?" He said, "I loosed from harbor. I pulled for the wreck with all my might. When I arrived, I loaded my boat until it was about to sink with women and children. I could not get one more aboard. Then I pulled for harbor, crying out, 'Oh, God, for a bigger boat'." That is the kind of praying you ought to do. Pray all the way to the house of the lost man. Win him to Jesus. Then pray all the way back, "Oh, God, for a bigger boat. Oh, God, for more ability. Oh, God, for more power. Oh, God, for more souls." We need to pray. But we need prayers with feet.

You are not going to see many folks saved unless you are willing to put feet to your prayers while you pray. I am supposed to get into the closet until I am endued with power. You say, "How do you know when you are endued with power?" The same way I know I got saved. If I am right with God the best way I know how, if my heart is clean, if I have confessed my sins, then I claim the power of God for soul winning, and I go. "How do you know you are saved?" Because God said so. I claimed the promise. I know it is true. That is how I know that I have the power of God when I go soul winning. I am not looking for a tingle up my spine. I do not wait for lightning to strike the building. I just get on my face and pray, "Oh, God, I need power."

You will be shocked to find out it does not take forever to get power if you are clean and you come to God asking Him for power to win souls and then go soul-winning. You will be shocked to find out that just a few minutes of praying and begging God for power and then going and using the power that you have will get the job done.

We pray for God to meet financial needs. Proverbs 19:17 says, *"He that hath pity upon the poor lendeth unto the LORD."* It does not say he that lendeth unto the poor. It says he that gives unto the poor. *"And that which he hath given will he pay him again"*, and I might add, with interest. God will always give back what you gave with interest. But let me stop to remind you that giving starts at eleven percent. The tithe belongs to God. You did not give the tithe, you paid it. That is your rent for breathing God's air and walking on His grass.

Giving begins at eleven percent. If you do not at least tithe, you certainly have not given anything to God. If you do not tithe, you are a thief. If you do not tithe, I am going to watch you around my billfold. If you will steal from God, you would steal from me.

We pray and say, "Oh, God. Meet the need. Old widow Jones down there, You know she does not have enough food to eat, and Oh, God, You know the building program at church. God, I pray You would bless and help them get the money for that building." You pray about all kinds of financial needs. Then you withhold your hand from giving. That is hypocritical praying. That is prayer with the feet cut off. Those are the kind you are not going to get an answer to. Those are the kind that are robbing God and robbing yourself of a blessing.

We say, "God, use somebody to meet the need. God, you saw that missionary. He needs a set of tires on his truck. Lord, I pray You would supply those tires." Do you think they are going to fall out of the sky? What you are praying is, "Lord, I am so sorry that I am not going to do anything, but I pray that You would touch somebody's heart to do something. What is mine is mine, but what is somebody else's You can use. Please do."

I believe in praying for finances. I believe in asking God to meet needs. It reminds me of the story of a little boy who was having devotions one night. His daddy was a deacon in the church. He was a good man, a moral man. He was faithful to the services three times a week. They had family devotions. They read the Bible that evening. They got down on their knees and his daddy prayed about many of the needs like I just mentioned. He prayed, "Oh, God. You know Mrs. Jones. You know she has financial needs. You know she does not have enough food. Lord, I pray that You would supply food for her and meet her need." Then he said, "Lord, You know that missionary that was just here last week needed a set of tires on his truck and God I pray You would supply the tires for him. Then Lord, the evangelist we have this week, I pray You would meet his financial needs. And Lord, You know the building fund down there is lagging a little bit. Lord, I pray You would supply the needs. Lord, You know the missionaries and all the needs they have. Oh, God, please meet the needs of the missionaries."

After they got through praying, his little boy got up off of his knees. He walked over and looked at his dad. He said, "Dad, I sure wish I had your money." "Why is that, son?" "Because if I had your money, I would answer your prayers!" Hey, if God had your money, He would answer your prayers, too. You want God to answer your prayers with someone else's money, that is your trouble. About half the financial needs you pray about, you could finance yourself, if you loved God enough to do it. If you would even initiate it, God would raise someone else up to the challenge. But you are praying about something you are not willing to contribute to yourself.

A preacher boy came by. He had a wife and a couple of kids. He had blown the engine in his car. He came by to visit me in Pennsylvania. When he stopped by, we talked for a few moments. He told me about his calamity. I said to him, "Well, son, come on in here and let's ask God to meet the need. " So we did. We went into my living room, got down on our knees and prayed. We said, "Oh, God, please. You know Steve needs a car. I pray You would supply the need. I pray You would give him a car." We prayed and got up off of our knees. By the way, I want you to know that God answered that prayer. But do you know whose car God gave him? God gave him my car. That was not what I had in mind. I wanted God to give him someone else's car. That is the way you pray too.

What we need are prayers with feet - our feet, our resources, our energy, our finances.

We pray for God to comfort the afflicted and strengthen the weak and encourage the discouraged and lift the fallen, but we are too busy to bother with them. You preachers think the ministry would be wonderful if it were not for all these cotton-pickin' people, wouldn't it? In case you did not know it, the ministry is people. It is not pretty sermons. It is people. It is not nice buildings. It is people. We pray for them and then we criticize them because God did not hit them with a boomerang and jerk them back when we prayed. We pray for the weak, and the afflicted, and the broken, and the fallen, and then we sit back and let them alone.

The Bible tells me about a wonderful friendship between Jonathan and David. The name Jonathan means "gift of Jehovah". The name David means "beloved". I want you to know that David was Jonathan's beloved friend, and Jonathan was a gift from God. Any true friend is a gift from God. Jonathan came and strengthened David's hand in the Lord. That is what a true friend will always do. Anyone who weakens your hand and your convictions and your service to God is not a friend. The Bible says Jonathan loved David as he loved his own soul. Now do not let these queers affect you. They try to make some kind of a perverted relationship out of it. This was true, loyal friendship, a bonding of souls, a spiritual friendship.

Both of these men were spiritual young men. Jonathan loved David as he loved his own soul. But he also loved God. Let me ask you a question. If you love somebody as much as you love your own soul, do you suppose you might pray for them? If Jonathan loved David as much as he loved his own soul, being a spiritual young man, do you suppose he might have prayed for him and for his prosperity and God's blessing on him? I am sure he did.

Jonathan did not stop with praying. There came a time when David became weak and weary, worn and tired. Jonathan left everything else behind and came to David's side. The Bible says that he strengthened his hand in the Lord.

You know, some of these people that you criticize and tear to shreds could be helped if you would just have time for them. If you had prayers with feet, if you sincerely poured your heart out to God and begged God to do something in their lives, then you took time to see what they needed and came to their side, you could pull a few of them out of the quagmire. You could help some of them. But we are too busy for that. We are too busy being big shots and being impressive for that. We do not have time for people. Why don't you get out of the ministry? Everybody is trying to decide who is qualified for the ministry but some of us who sit in judgment of everybody else do not practice the ministry anyway.

I believe in pastoral leadership. But we have taken it so far that we are big shots and sit upon a throne and everybody else is supposed to kiss our toes like we were the pope. My job as a preacher is to minister, to help. If I do not have time for people, I ought to go get an honest job. Folks need somebody to minister to them and love them. They need for us to pray, but to have prayers with feet.

I was in a revival meeting in northeast Pennsylvania. I was preaching for a young fellow and he said, "Hey, Brother Corle. I want you to pray for Brother ____. He has just been through a bad church split. He is heartbroken. Some awful things have been done and said. He is discouraged." I said, "Okay, I will do that."

For two days I prayed for him. On the third day, I

said, "What is that guy's phone number? I want to give
him a call." He said, "You do not know him, do you?" I
said, "No." He said, "Okay, I will give it to you." He gave
me the phone number. I called that fellow. He answered
the phone and I started talking to him. He was as low as
a snake's belly in a wagon rut. He was having trouble. I
said, "This is Brother Corle. You do not know me. But we
have a mutual friend. He told me what you had been
through and I just felt like I needed to call. I just wanted
you to know that I am praying for you. I want to
encourage you to hang in there. God is going to do
something great there. I believe that is why the devil is
fighting. Just hang on."

A couple years ago I held him a meeting. In seven
days we had one hundred and seventy-five saved and
eighty-three baptized. He is still there. I have held him
several meetings like that since that time when I gave
him that phone call. I hardly ever preach for the guy but
that he does not walk up to the pulpit and look back all
teary-eyed with his lip quivering. He will say, "You just
do not know, brother. You do not have any idea what that
phone call meant."

He is right. I did not know. I did not know
whether I could encourage him or not. I just knew that
God wanted me to call him and talk to him. I was
praying for him and God said, "Put some feet on those
prayers." I gave the guy a call and talked to him for a few
minutes. Who knows but that God did not keep him
there because of that. I am not taking the credit. To God
be the glory. He is the one who told me to do it.

The trouble is, we are not obedient to the Spirit of
God when He moves on our hearts. We are too busy. I
thank God for every Christian that calls my name out in
prayer, but I am especially thankful to every one that has
prayers with feet. They not only pray for me but they

come to my side when I am struggling and need encouragement and help, when I am under attack. I have been, and will be, and so will you, if you continue to do anything for God.

We need prayers with feet - our feet. When we see somebody that is down, we need to go ahead and pray for him, and then go lift him up while we are praying. If we see somebody that is discouraged, we need to go ahead and pray for him, and then encourage him while we pray. If we see somebody that is backslidden, we need to go get them by the arm and lead them back to the right way while we pray for them.

I heard a preacher tell about a bad storm. He had a small son at that time. He said that the lightning was flashing, and the thunder was roaring, and the limbs of the trees were scratching against the windows. Every time the lightning would flash, those shadows would go across the room. At one o'clock in the morning the preacher heard his son whimpering and crying. He got up out of bed and went over into his son's bedroom, patted him on the back and said, "Son, it is okay. It is all right." He prayed with him. After he prayed with him, he said, "Now son, it is all right. Jesus is with you." He said his little boy rolled over and looked up at him and said, "I know that, Dad. But tonight, I need someone with skin on him."

Hey, when people are down they do not need pious platitudes. They need a Christian who will come to their side. They are discouraged. They need an encourager. While you pray, go and encourage them. They need someone with skin on them, not just pious platitudes.

Brother, you wait until you are in the same shape as some of the people to whom you say, "Well, the Lord is with you." And then you do not understand why they are still upset.

We pray for God to send laborers and then we never even consider ourselves as a prospect, as one of the laborers. We just better get back to the real stuff.

I hold meetings with preachers who are too busy in the ministry to go soulwinning. They say, "I do not know why I cannot get any soulwinners." Because you do not attract what you want, you attract what you are. And you are not a soulwinner. You say, "Well, all those people you got stirred up about soulwinning, as soon as you left they quit." I know, because you will not go. You cannot send them soulwinning; you must take them.

"Then saith he unto his disciples, The harvest truly is scarce. Hardly anybody wants to get saved." Is that what He said? *"The harvest truly is plenteous, but the labourers are few."* Then watch what He did. He said, *"Pray ye therefore the Lord of the harvest,"* that He will save sinners, is that what He said? He said, *"Pray ye therefore the Lord of the harvest, that he will send forth labourers into his harvest."* He said, "Pray for labourers." The first thing Jesus did was show His disciples the need. Then He called them to prayer. He said, "Look at the need. Let's pray about the need, okay? Let's pray for God to send forth labourers into the harvest."

In Luke 10:1 look what He did. Boy, was He tricky. *"And when he had called unto him his twelve disciples, he gave them power against unclean spirits, to cast them out, and to heal all manner of sickness and all manner of disease."* The first thing He did was show them a need. The next thing He did was have them pray about the need. The next thing He did was give them power. While they prayed, He equipped them and empowered them to meet the need.

But He did not stop there. *"These twelve* (the same twelve He showed the need, the same twelve He instructed to pray, the same twelve He empowered) *Jesus sent forth, and commanded them, saying, Go not into the way of the Gentiles, and into any city of the Samaritans enter ye not: But go rather to the lost sheep of the house of Israel." (Luke 10:5).* The first thing He did was show them a need and get a burden on their heart. Then He told them to pray about the need. While they were praying He changed them. Did you know that Jesus did not change the lost world in answer to the disciples' prayer? He changed them in answer to their prayer and they changed the lost world.

Psalm 10:17 says, *"Lord, thou hast heard the desire of the humble: thou wilt prepare their heart, thou wilt cause thine ear to hear."* God puts a burden on my heart. Then He causes me to pray. While I am praying, God changes me. Then God uses me to meet the need that I prayed about. That is what He will do with you, too, if you are available. I am not ruling out the supernatural answers. We have covered that. I am talking about the fact that most of your prayers are going to be in these two categories of putting feet to them.

Moses prayed for a deliverer. Guess who God sent. Moses! William Carey began to pray for the conversion of the heathen world. Guess who God sent. David Brainerd began to pray for the conversion of the American Indians. Guess who God sent. You are right. He sent the guy that He burdened to pray about it. What He wanted to do when He burdened that man to prayer was change the man so the man would change the situation. Many of the things God gives you a burden for and causes you to pray about, instead of Him changing the circumstances in answer to your prayer, He is going to change you in answer to your prayer and you will change those circumstances. That is, if you have prayers with feet.

The Jewish general, Allenby, who took Jerusalem

back from the Turks in 1917 without firing a shot, is a Jewish hero. When asked about the situation later, he said, "From the time I was a small boy, my mother gave me a prayer to pray every day. I prayed this prayer as a boy and all through my childhood - 'Oh, Lord. We would not forget Thy ancient people, Israel. Hasten the day when Israel shall again be Thy people, and shall be restored again to Thy favor in their land.' " After the war he said, "I never thought God would allow me to have a part in the answer to my own childhood prayers." He prayed for them to be restored and made himself available as an instrument and God performed it. He had prayers with feet.

   We need to pray for the work of the ministry, but when we do that we need to have prayers with feet and be available. We need to pray for sinners to be saved, but we need prayers with feet. We need to go soulwinning. We need to pray for the needs of others financially, and the needs of the church financially, and the needs of evangelists and missionaries. We need to pray. But we need prayers with feet - our feet. We need to pray for God to comfort the afflicted and strengthen the weak and lift the fallen but we need to be a comforter and a strengthener and a lifter and a restorer while we pray. We need to pray for laborers and then surrender to be one of them.

   There was a man who lived in the time of Martin Luther. His name was Miconias. Martin Luther went out single-handedly to fight corruption. (Let me mention once again that I am a Baptist, not a Reformer. But I do have some admiration for these men who were at least sincere enough to fight the corruption and not go along with it.)   Martin Luther decided that he was going to fight the corruption in the Catholic church. He took his Ninety-Nine Theses and nailed it on the door at Wittenberg at the Council of Worms, and got into a big fuss. Miconias came to him before he undertook that endeavor and said, "Martin, I am sympathetic to your cause. I am for everything that you are for. I am against everything you are against. I am for you in the fight but I can do no greater thing than to abide at home and pray for thee."

Martin Luther went out single-handedly to do the work. Miconias was sympathetic, but stayed at home and did nothing but pray. One night Miconias was sleeping. In the middle of the night he had a dream. He dreamed of a single reaper out in the field with literally thousands upon thousands of acres to be reaped. That one man was out there in the hot sun with a hand scythe. He cleared off a small area. He was weak, and weary, about to fall in the work. As Miconias dreamed, that man, that reaper, turned and began to walk toward him, and he saw the face of Martin Luther, about to fall in the labor.

Miconias woke up in a cold sweat and sat up in the bed. He said, "It is not enough that I should pray. Fields need harvested. Sheep need shepherded. Souls need saved. Sermons need preached. Here am I, Lord. Send me."

We have a lot of people who tell us, "I am sympathetic to what you are for, Preacher. But I can do no greater thing than to abide at home and pray for thee." Oh, yes you can. You can go soulwinning and pray for me while you are soulwinning with me. You can reach down into your billfold and give sacrificially while you are praying for the need. You can teach a class while you are praying for God to meet the needs and bless the church. You can have prayers with feet, which are far better than prayers with the feet cut off. We desperately need prayers with feet.

Do you even pray? How much time and effort and energy do you spend in prayer to start with? Do you have prayers with feet or are you praying and then cutting the feet off of your prayers? God teach us to pray and then put feet to our prayers.

CHAPTER EIGHT

PREVAILING PRAYER

There never has been a great revival without much praying. There have been some great revivals without much preaching. Evan Roberts was not a dynamic preacher, but he got people together for prayer meetings and the Welsh Revival was born as a result of it.

God answers prayer. But God's people spend far too little time in the prayer closet. We speak a great deal about praying and still do very little of it. James 5:15-18 says, *"And the prayer of faith shall save the sick, and the Lord shall raise him up; and if he have committed sins, they shall be forgiven him. Confess your faults one to another, and pray one for another, that ye may be healed. The effectual fervent prayer of a righteous man availeth much. Elias was a man subject to like passions as we are, and he prayed earnestly that it might not rain: and it rained not on the earth by the space of three years and six months. And he prayed again, and the heaven gave rain, and the earth brought forth her fruit."*

Some folks would look at this promise and say, "Well, that was for the Jews only. That was for another generation." But there are many things that stand out that prove that this is not so. We will look at that in a moment.

History tells us of many who prevailed in prayer. He said, *"The effectual fervent prayer of a righteous man availeth much."* There is a lot of learning in that verse. It is not just, "If we go ahead and pray a little God will answer our prayers." That is not what it says there. But the Word of God gives us story after story after story where folks paid the price in the prayer closet and prevailed. The power of God came down.

Jacob became Israel, a prince with God and a prince with man because he prevailed, praying all night long, wrestling with the angel all night long. Elijah is mentioned in chapter five of the Book of James. The Bible says he prayed and the rain stopped because of his prayer.

I once heard Dr. Hyles talk about John R. Rice. He said they were in a conference somewhere. It was an open pavilion with just poles and a roof on it. Dr. Hyles got up to preach. He read his text and a terrible rainstorm came up. He said he looked over and Dr. Rice had stepped outside. He raised his hands up and began to pray. The rain stopped. Brother Hyles finished his sermon. Dr. Rice came in with that little ornery, boyish grin of his. He looked at him and he said, "Dr. Hyles. It is my turn to preach. Your turn to stop the rain." He was a man of prayer. He was a man who walked with God. He had power with God. He believed God could do it and would do it. He prevailed in prayer.

We need some folks like that in our generation. We need some people who pray and get answers. We need some folks who know what it means to get an answer from God, a definite answer, an immediate answer, because they did not just start praying when a problem came up. They had been praying all along, prevailing in prayer.

Elijah was no different than you or me, neither was John Rice. Dr. Boyd is a great man of prayer. I have seen him prevail in prayer. I have prayed with him many times. He prays about everything. It does not matter what happens. He says, "Son, let's pray." I like that. There are not many folks in that state of mind anymore.

Charles Finney said when the great revivals were

breaking out all over the land, God's people came together and would simply fall on their faces. They did not stand around and fellowship. They never got into any gossip because they came together as soon as they met and fellowshipped in prayer. They fell on their faces and began to walk with God and pray and plead for souls and plead for revival and pray for power. Many of them would pray all night long. New converts prayed until they were nearly without strength.

One old man travelled with Finney. He said the great success that he had in his revival meetings was due mostly to that old man's prayers. He said he would pray with such fervency that he would sweat and strain and cry out to God. He would pray from morning until afternoon. He would be so weak and so tired from straining and struggling in prayer that he could not even come to the meetings. He would just collapse and have to go to bed and rest. He would get up the next morning and walk with God.

Prayer affects eternity. Someone has to prevail in the prayer closet. God can do a lot more with the hearts of men than you and I can. We need to bring it to Him and plead with Him.

In the Book of Samuel Hannah began to pray. She had been barren for a long time, but she pleaded with God, "Oh, God, I have to have a son." She was weeping and sobbing and crying, so much so that Eli thought she was drunk. He rebuked her but she said, "My lips are moving but no sound is coming out because my heart is heavy. My heart is broken. I am barren." He said, "The Lord give thee thy request." She got that son she had labored over and prayed for, but she made God a promise. She said, "If You will give me a son, I will give him back." And she did exactly what she promised God. Hannah prevailed in prayer.

Daniel, after twenty-one days of fasting, prevailed in prayer. There he was, on his face praying. The Bible says that the devil and the forces of hell held up the angel that was coming with the answer. Now, if that had been most of us, it would have been all over. We would have quit praying before the twenty-one days were up. We would have stopped fasting and praying and pleading with God. We would have said, "Well, I guess God just does not want me to have it."

D.L. Moody said, "Most people who pray are like little boys at Halloween. They knock on a door and run and all they are is an aggravation. By the time somebody gets to the door they have already flown." That is the way most people pray. They do not know anything about prevailing. They do not know anything about *"Ask, and it shall be given you; seek, and ye shall find; knock, and it shall be opened unto you."* That means "ask, and keep on asking; seek, and keep on seeking; knock, and keep on knocking." God will keep on answering as a result of it.

Daniel prevailed after twenty-one days of fasting. He finally got the victory. The answer finally came. But it did not come in his timing.

Do you know what God is doing to us many times when He makes us pray and pray and pray? We could not handle the answer if we got it. God is getting us earnest enough about our prayer so that when the answer comes we will not take it lightly, so that we will give Him glory for it, and we will care for the answer.

Many of us pray for things that would not be good for us right now because our hearts are not prepared and ready to receive it. If we got the answer it would not be a blessing. It would be our ruin. God knows that. So God makes us prevail in prayer in order to get the answer. Prevailing in prayer prepares my heart.

Hezekiah prevailed as he turned his face to the wall. Isaiah came in and said, "Set your house in order. You are going to die." He went back out and got to the bottom of the steps going out of the courtyard. The Lord said, "I want you to turn around." Why did God do that? As soon as Isaiah walked out of the room, Hezekiah turned his face to the wall. He began to weep and plead with God. God said to Isaiah, "You go back and tell Hezekiah I have heard his prayer and seen his tears. I have added fifteen years to the days of his life." God answered his prayer. He prevailed.

The early church got together. Can you imagine the unbelievable message they had to carry to a lost and dying world? They had to go out and tell somebody that they had a Jesus that lived a perfect life and never sinned. Then they had to convince them that Christ died for everybody's sins and paid for all of them, not just past sins, but future sins. That is pretty unbelievable. Then they had to convince them that not only did He die for sin, but He arose from the dead. If that was not bad enough, they had to convince them that He ascended up to heaven in a body of flesh and bones. No wonder they prayed for ten days.

We are trying to tell the same story. We need the same power. The Gospel is an unbelievable story unless we prevail in prayer. They prayed for ten days in perfect unity and the power of God fell. They came out of that upper room as a whirlwind for God. Three thousand saved, three thousand baptized, three thousand added to the local church at Jerusalem, all in one day. They prevailed in prayer.

What happened on the day of Pentecost was not the result of one man's sermon. It was the result of one hundred and twenty Spirit-filled soulwinners doing the work, as well as that sermon. That sermon did not get

everybody saved. Everybody was soulwinning. They
were doing the work. It was not just Peter.

Paul and Silas prevailed in Acts chapter sixteen.
When they prayed God shook the jail house and opened
the doors. Everyone's bands were loosed. When did you
ever see an earthquake that did nothing but open doors?
That was no natural earthquake. God said, "I am going
to answer their prayer and show that jailor they belong to
Me. Then he will get saved." They prevailed in prayer
and God honored their prayer. He shook the place.

In Acts chapter twelve you will find a band of
Christians rather discouraged. Their leaders had just
been taken. James had been killed with the sword. Peter
had been placed in jail. They were gathered in a house
having a secret prayer meeting, hoping that no one would
burst in on them. They were rather distraught and
discouraged. There they were, praying, pleading for God
to get Peter out of jail.

I like this story, because it shows that if I just have
microscopic faith, God will still answer prayer. It is not
big faith that gets prayers answered. It is mustard seed
faith, just a little bit.

They kept on praying and kept on praying. When
Peter came they said, "It cannot be him. He is in jail."
Rhoda said, "Yes, it is him." "No, it must be his angel. It
could not be him. He is in jail." Finally they came out
and checked and said, "What are you doing here? You are
supposed to be in jail." They got their prayer answered.
They prevailed in prayer. Not because they had great
faith, but because they had a little bit of faith and they
kept at it. They just kept praying.

I heard Brother Hyles preach a sermon and in that
sermon he talked about "I know, I think." "I know it is
going to happen, I think." "I know God can answer my
prayer, I think." What he was saying was that all of us

have a little bit of apprehension, a grain of salt, a little bit of doubt in there at times. But if we have enough faith to ask and keep on asking and keep on asking and keep on asking, God is going to answer.

George Mueller prayed down seven million dollars. That would probably be seven billion dollars in our generation. He never told anyone what he needed. He built his orphan homes on prayer. He prayed for food and set the table and a milk wagon would break down out in front of the church on a hot day. The driver would say, "Mr. Mueller, my milk and my cheese are going to spoil. Could you use it?" He had the table set, waiting for it to break down. He did not know where it was coming from, but he prayed and prevailed.

Once George Mueller was on a ship going to a speaking engagement. As he neared the harbor the captain told him, "With all this fog we will never get there on time. We are going to be held up for at least another day or two. You will miss your speaking engagement." Mueller said, "I have never missed a speaking engagement, and by the grace of God I will not miss this one."

He said, "Come with me down to the hull of the ship and we will pray. We will ask God to lift the fog." The fellow said, "It is no use." Mueller said, "Never mind. Do not even pray. I will pray. But come with me." He said, "I do not want you to pray if you do not believe God is going to do something."

They went down into the hull of the ship. Mueller prayed, and when they came back up on deck the fog had already lifted. God had answered prayer and he made it in plenty of time for his speaking engagement.

We do not use one of the greatest assets that God gave us. One of the greatest resources a child of God has we let lie dormant and do not use. The mighty power of God is available and we can tap it by prevailing in prayer.

God is not going to pour His power out on us for a play thing. He is not going to bless us to exalt our flesh. When we come to God properly and prevail the answer will come. George Mueller cited fifty thousand definite answers to prayer in his lifetime. He was a man of prayer.

John Hyde literally prayed himself to death at the ripe old age of twenty-nine. So did David Brainerd. So did Payson. Many others literally prayed themselves to death, walking with God. But they probably accomplished more in the prayer closet in that brief twenty-nine years, they probably had more lasting results and fruit for eternity in prevailing prayer than most of us will accomplish if we live to be seventy-five or eighty because we do not pray and we do not affect eternity. Prevailing prayer is so important.

John Knox cried out, "Give me Scotland or I die." God gave him Scotland. Muncy said, "Oh, God, give me souls or take my soul." He prevailed. God gave him literally thousands of souls.

John Hyde prayed for one convert a day to be saved and baptized. God gave him one convert a day. Then for two, and then for three and then for four, and for the latter days of his life every day God gave him four converts. But he prayed them down.

There was an old man in my home town. He was a precious man. One of the finest Christians I know, a great prayer warrior. He never was a preacher. He was just a godly layman. He visited his bus route, but he said to me, "I could miss visiting, spend the three hours in prayer, and fill that bus up." I do not suggest that anyone skip their visiting, because God intended for us to do both. But the man said, "If I had to skip praying to visit, I would skip visiting and pray." God is still the same today as He was back in the days of James.

In Psalm 65:2 the Bible says, *"O thou that hearest prayer, unto thee shall all flesh come."* God is the God that answers prayer. He identifies Himself as the only one who does, by the way. Baal does not answer prayer. Molech does not answer prayer. But Jehovah God does answer prayer.

In Hebrews 13:8 the Bible says, *"Jesus Christ the same yesterday, and to day, and for ever."* Any promise in the Bible is still available to me. In Jeremiah 33:3 He said, *"Call unto me, and I will answer thee, and shew thee great and mighty things, which thou knowest not."* I like claiming that. I get a charge out of these folks that say, "That tithing. That is under the law of the Old Testament." But they do not mind claiming Jeremiah 33:3, do they? All of it is for us.

Vance Havner said that some theologian heard him praying and claiming Jeremiah 33:3. The fella told him, "No, that promise is to the Jews. That is not for this dispensation. That is not for you. You cannot get prayers answered on that." He said, "Well, bless God. I just learned something. I have been getting prayers answered on that for fifty years and I just found out it is not for me."

Malachi 3:6 says, *"For I am the LORD, I change not; therefore ye sons of Jacob are not consumed."* Why? Because God made them a promise. The only reason He had not consumed them is because He is an eternal God and He made an eternal promise. He never changes.

Gentiles are made a whole lot like Jews are. They have a head and two arms and two legs. They are sinners too. I do not think God holds it against us Gentiles for claiming a Jewish promise, especially one that has to do with prayer. God would be excited if we claimed anything and just prayed a little bit. Again and again the Bible tells us that God is still the same today as He was then. He is still today the God that answers prayer.

Sometimes good men will say of James chapter five, "That is for a past dispensation." Do not believe it for a minute. It is not true. Look what it says in James 5:3. *"Your gold and silver is cankered; and the rust of them shall be a witness against you, and shall eat your flesh as it were fire. Ye have heaped treasure together for the last days."* Look at verse eight. *"Be ye also patient; stablish your hearts: for the coming of the Lord draweth nigh."* This promise is for the last days. It is for just prior to the coming of the Lord. Notice verse nine. *"Grudge not one against another, brethren, lest ye be condemned: behold, the judge standeth before the door."* It is talking again about the coming of the Lord Jesus. This is not for some past dispensation.

The rest of the chapter gives the promises that God gave for prayer. God still answers prayer today. God still heals bodies. I am not talking about all the trickery and fakery that goes on today. You have seen that crowd. Where I come from they do not call that prayer. They call that karate. I would make a good faith healer. I have a good right. I can knock them out and wait till they come to and tell everybody they got healed. God said if someone is sick, call for the elders of the church. Ask those men to come and pray for you.

God gave us Elijah as a model. He was a man who got his prayers answered, but he was still human and got backslidden a little bit later. In one place he prevailed in prayer, and in another place he got discouraged and quit the ministry. He said, "Oh, God, kill me. I want to die." He defeated eight hundred and fifty prophets and ran from one woman. Of course, Jezebel would be enough to scare anybody.

I want you to notice something about the prayer that God says prevails. James 5:15, *"And the prayer of faith shall save the sick, and the Lord shall raise him up; and if he have committed sins, they shall be forgiven him."* It is **expecting prayer**, expecting God to do something, trusting God to do something, believing God is able to do something. Prayer without faith is not really prayer. It is just muttering words. Anything in the Christian life without faith does not amount to much. Faith is the foundation and the springboard for everything in the Christian life. We are saved by faith and we live by faith and walk by faith and get answers to prayer by faith.

This prevailing prayer is expecting prayer. Faith is not just believing that God can, but that God will. Anybody can say, "I believe God can," but the ones who get their prayers answered say, "I not only believe He can, I believe He will."

I hear women sometimes talk about their husbands. No wonder they do not get saved. "Why, you do not want to go see him. He will not get saved. It is no use. You may as well forget it. He will never come to church. He will not talk to anybody." Boy, aren't you an inspiration? You do not believe God is big enough to save him. He can save an old murderer like Paul, but He cannot save your unsaved loved one. He could not save your daddy. He could not save your mother. He could not save your uncle. He could not save your husband. He could not save your brother. God could not answer your prayer for them. Oh, yes. He could save Paul. Yes, He could save the jailor. Yes, He could save the maniac of Gadara, demon possessed. He could save an old, cussing fisherman like Peter, but He could not save your husband, huh? You do not think much of Him, do you?

God, through prayer, is able to save people. But

you are going to have to come to God expecting Him to do something, believing that He can and that He will. We look at things too humanly many times, too skeptically. We forget there is a supernatural God. We compare God to us and because we cannot accomplish something, we just give up on it and do not pray about it. We figure if we cannot do it, God cannot do it either. That is where you are wrong, friend. When you and I come to the end of ourselves and there is no more that we can do, then God is ready to get involved. He rolls His sleeves up and with the power of His might accomplishes what no man can do.

Notice something in the first part of James 5:16 about prevailing prayer. He said, *"Confess your faults one to another."* It is not only expecting prayer, but **eschewing prayer**. Do you remember what God said about Job? He said, *"There is none like him in the earth, a perfect and an upright man, one that feareth God, and escheweth evil." (Job 1:8)* What did Job do? He kept evil away from him. He had no desire for it. He prayed and confessed.

If you and I are going to get our prayers answered, if we expect God to do something, we need to come honestly, clearing our record. The Bible says, *"If I regard iniquity in my heart, the Lord will not hear me." (Psalm 66:18)* That means if I have sin in my heart that no one else knows about, just me, and I come to God asking for things, if I harbor sin in my heart and do not get it out I am not going to get my prayers answered.

We need two kinds of righteousness to get our prayers answered. First is imputed righteousness. Unsaved people are not going to get their prayers answered. "Well, what about that fella Cornelius in Acts chapter ten?" All God did was send somebody by because he had an open heart. If a person has an open heart and is honestly searching with all the light he has, God will send a soulwinner by his house too.

The Bible tells me I nèed imputed righteousness. I need to be saved first, then I need personal righteousness. I need to be separated from sin and confess my sin.

The Bible talks about confession of sin in I John 1:9. It says, *"If we confess our sins, he is faithful and just to forgive us our sins, and to cleanse us from all unrighteousness."* If we say the same thing about our sin that God says about it He will forgive and cleanse. He said if I have the same attitude about my sin, and hate my sin like God hates it, and talk about it like God talks about it, and confess it and shun it like God shuns it, then He will cleanse me of that sin and forgive me of all unrighteousness.

If I will honestly and sincerely repent of my sin and get it right with God, if I will confess and forsake what I know is wrong with me, God will forgive me for what I do not know is wrong with me. He will cleanse me from all unrighteousness.

So many times we are too pious to get an answer to prayer. If you will notice, it was not only confession to God but confession to one another. I am not talking about giving all the details of your past sins. I am just saying you ought to be humble enough to use an altar and publicly admit that you have a need. Some folks want everybody to think they have arrived. That is why they will not use the altar. That is why they will not walk the aisle. They want everybody else to think that they are such great Christians that they do not need the altar. If you are such a great Christian that you do not need the altar you ought to be in heaven. None of us has arrived.

One key to prevailing prayer is to call on the Lord out of a pure heart. That is what Paul told Timothy in II Timothy 2:22, to call on the Lord out of a pure heart, having your faults confessed, and unashamed to fall on an altar and confess to others that you have fallen short of the glory of God, that you have failed, that you have done wrong.

You will find a big list of people in the Bible who all said, "I have sinned." I like what David said, *"Against thee, thee only, have I sinned."* He did not just stop with, "I have sinned," but he said, "I have sinned against God Almighty." What an awful thing. Every time we sin, we sin against God Almighty.

Notice what James said in verse 16. *"The effectual fervent prayer of a righteous man availeth much."* That is **effective prayer**, that which is practical and effective.

Unless the heart of desire moves the lips of petition, we pray without purpose. These old, cold, hard, dead, formal, beautiful, flowery prayers do not amount to a hill of beans. God wants someone with a hot heart who comes along and really wants an answer, someone who comes in earnest, someone who comes effectually.

It is not the arithmetic of our prayers that gets them answered - how many. Nor the rhetoric of our prayers - how eloquent. It is not the geometry of our prayers - how long they are. It is not the music of our prayers - how sweet the noise. I hear people say sometimes, "Oh, that was a pretty prayer." There is nothing wrong with a prayer sounding pretty, but if that is all it was, then God help us. I'd rather hear some fella slobber and growl and snarl in prayer that was not pretty at all but it got to Glory and brought down the power.

It is not the logic of our prayers - how argumentative, but a fervent spirit *"availeth much"*, the Bible says.

I remember reading about Wilbur Chapman. He was holding a revival in London. He had heard much about John Hyde. He had hoped to meet him some day.

While Chapman was holding a revival, John Hyde walked in. He said, "When he walked into the service, there was something different about the entire service." The little old man sat down in the back. As Chapman preached he could see and feel the conviction of God falling on the entire place.

He finished preaching and eighteen people came forward and got saved. Nobody had been saved the night before. He asked the pastor beside him, "Who is that man?" The pastor said, "That is John Hyde."

Hyde got Chapman and took him to a side room after the service. He knelt down to pray with him. Chapman said that he listened to the old man, the masterful prayer warrior. He lifted his hands up in the air with tears streaming from both of his eyes and he said, "Oh, God." Then two minutes of silence passed without another word, as though he were waiting for the very presence of God to settle on the place. He said it was as real as the dew settling on the ground when the presence of God settled into the room. Then he continued to pour out his heart to God in prayer, pleading, praying.

> Prayer is the soul's sincere desire
> Uttered, or unexpressed.
> The motion of a hidden fire
> That trembles in our breast.

Real prayer is spawned in the heart, not the head. Real prayer comes from the depths of the soul. Most of what we do is what Jesus rebuked in Matthew chapter six as vain repetition. There is no fervency of spirit, no effectual earnestness in our soul, no driving force within. Without fervency, prayer is not even beginning to be effectual or effective in our lives.

In James 5:17 the Bible says it was **earnest**

prayer. What that word really means is that he prayed with much praying. He prayed with prayer. How about that? He just earnestly prayed and prayed and prayed and prayed. That is what old John Rice said, "Prayer is asking and receiving." Not just asking, but asking and receiving. That is what real prayer is.

When we talk about earnestness, we are talking about straining, wrestling with God. The same as Jacob at Peniel when he wrestled with God and came forth with the mighty power of God on his life, a changed man. It cost him something though. He limped the rest of his days. The hollow of his thigh was touched. The sinew shrank. It costs something to get a prayer answered. God does not have any discounts on answered prayer. He does not have any blue light specials. It costs something to get prayer answered and someone has to care enough to labor in prayer and sweat in prayer and weep in the prayer closet.

When I see a fella preach, I like to see him sweat a little bit. When I see a fella pray for any length of time in an all night prayer meeting, I like to see somebody sweat a little bit in prayer. I like to hear them cry out a little bit in prayer. God will not be offended if you get a little bit excited in the prayer closet and lose some of your dignity. He will not be offended if you cry out from the depths of your soul, hungry, starving, for some kind of power to fall.

The word "supplication" means "praying with sweat." David Brainerd died at age twenty-nine. Many who have read his life's story have had their lives changed. Robert Murray McCheyne read Brainerd's life's story and was transformed into a great prayer warrior. David Brainerd would pray in the middle of winter for the Indians with such fervor and intensity that he would melt snow for six feet around his body.

Once, when Brainerd was praying, the Indians were sneaking in for an attack. He was on his face, interceding for them. As they moved in about to kill him, they noticed that a rattlesnake was crawling toward him. There he was, kneeling, lifeless, pouring out his soul to God. The Indians had decided that the gods were going to destroy him and this snake was one of the gods coming to get him out of their presence. But when the snake came to him it simply lifted its head and crawled over the back of his leg and kept going. When the Indians saw that they befriended him and received him as a great man. He prayed earnestly. He prayed with sweat. He labored.

In James 5:17 the Bible says we need to pray **explicit prayer**, for exactly what we want. *"He prayed earnestly that it might not rain: and it rained not."* Most folks pray, "God bless all the missionaries. Bless everyone. Save the world." If we ever got a prayer answered we would not know it. If God ever blessed anybody, we would not know we had anything to do with it. God wants us to learn to pray in specifics. If I need a thousand dollars, I am not going to say, "Dear Lord, please give me a little money." I am going to say, "God, I need a thousand dollars."

When I came to my daddy I did not say, "Now I lay me down to sleep, I need a dollar." I came to my dad and said, "Dad, I need five dollars. I have to put gas in the car." I had to come and ask specifically for what I wanted.

Elijah prayed that it might not rain and it did not rain. He prayed that it would and it did. He prayed for fire to fall and it came down.

Lavinnia Holoman was a little black lady in my home town. She was a widow. She was one of the finest, sweetest Christians I have known. She did not have much, but she literally walked with God and lived by way of prayer.

I remember once she stood and gave a testimony. She had been out of food for a couple of days. She began to pray. One morning, as she had the kitchen window open she got down on her knees in front of the kitchen sink and she began to pray. She prayed for some soup and she prayed for some potatoes and she prayed for some bread and some peanut butter. She prayed through a whole order. She told God exactly what she wanted.

It just so happened that while she was praying three ornery teenage boys came by the window and heard her praying. They decided they were going to play a practical joke on her. They wrote down everything she said. They went to the store and bought exactly what she prayed for. They brought it to the door and knocked. They thought she was going to be surprised, but they got the surprise. She said, "Praise the Lord. I knew you would get them here today, God." It shocked the fire out of those boys.

You say, "Well, that is just a coincidence." Oh, yeah? God answered her prayer through those boys. If she had prayed like some of you pray she would still be hungry.

We need to learn to pray explicitly. I remember talking to an old skeptic down in North Carolina. I took my wife to the laundromat one morning. I started witnessing to this fella. He said, "I do not believe all that stuff." He started giving me all this scientific stuff. I said, "Let me ask you something. If there is no God and the Bible is not true, answer me one question." He was all ready. He had all his scientific answers together. I said, "How is it that I got seventy definite answers to prayer in the last ninety days?"

He said, "That is just coincidence." I said, "I'll tell

you what I will do. In the next ninety days, I will take fifty things I need for my ministry and things I want. I will not tell anybody but God. You take fifty things you want. You tell anybody you want to. Write everybody you want to. Call everybody you want to. I will compare notes with you at the end of ninety days and see who got what they needed." He would not take me up on it. One thing a skeptic cannot argue with is answered prayer. The infidel can come up with his philosophies and his arguments, but he cannot argue with the mighty power of God meeting our needs in answer to definite, explicit prayer.

That same week I prayed down a car. I did not tell anyone. I was in a car with a preacher out soulwinning. I had been praying for a car for two months to tow along behind our motorhome. I had been praying for a straight stick. I prayed for a small car, four cylinder. I was out soulwinning with a preacher. He looked over at me and said, "How do you like this car?" I said, "It is a nice little car." He said, "You could probably use one like this, couldn't you?" I said, "Yeah, we could use something like this." He said, "Well, my wife and I have been praying about it, and we believe God wants us to give you this car. If you will take it, we want to give it to you."

Argue all you want to. I know there is a God up there.

I was praying for a paper folder. We needed one for the office. Hand-folding was a big job. I was in Arkansas. I went into a room with a preacher. He said, "Do you know what that is? It is a paper folder." I said, "Really? Is that what that is?" He said, "Yeah. About a month ago, someone broke into the church and tried to steal it. It was heavy and they dropped it. The insurance company, instead of fixing it, just bought us a new one. Do you suppose you could use one of them?" I said, "Yeah,

I think I could." I had been praying for that for a month.

I am praying for some things right now. We prayed for computers and God gave them to us. We prayed for a secretary and God gave me one of my own converts from our home church who had just finished some secretarial training. God is able and He will answer prayer.

We get prayers answered all the time. God gave us our truck and trailer. God is good. He answers prayer, but it takes a while. I am praying for some things right now that I will guarantee you God is going to give us because we are going to use them for the glory of God and He knows that. We will have them.

When we need something we ask God for it. I am not timid. I am not afraid to ask God for something. I ask Him for the big things and for the little things and everything in between.

Then we see in James 5:18 **enduring prayer**. *"He prayed again."* This time he prayed for rain. *"The heaven gave rain."* There needs to be a continuing in our prayer. In Acts 2:42 the Bible says, *"And they continued stedfastly in the apostles' doctrine and fellowship, and in breaking of bread, and in prayers."* There was a stedfastness in their prayer lives. Most Christians are very inconsistent, up and down, back and forth, on and off. There is no consistency in prayer. They do not pray as they should and because of it they never develop the kind of prayer life that they need to see God constantly pouring out His blessings.

Verse eighteen is the clincher to the whole matter, **God-exalting prayer**. *"And he prayed again, and the heaven gave rain, and the earth brought forth fruit."* We need to pray to the glory of God. We need to pray and when God answers, God needs to get the glory out of our prayers.

God created us for His glory. *"The heavens*

declare the glory of God; and the firmament sheweth his handiwork." God said in the Psalms, *"Call upon me in the day of trouble; I will answer thee, and thou shalt glorify me."* God says my prayers ought to glorify Him. God answers prayer to His own glory.

God will do the miraculous if your motive is to glorify Him. God will do the miraculous in response to your prayer if your motive is to honor Christ and to save the lost and to glorify God. God-exalting prayer makes all the difference.

One great man, when asked what the secret of his success was said, *"Ask, and ye shall receive; seek, and ye shall find; knock, and it shall be opened to you. For everyone that asketh receiveth; he that seeketh findeth; to him that knocketh it shall be opened."* He said, "Ask, and keep on asking. God will keep on answering."

This prevailing prayer that we are talking about is expecting prayer. It is eschewing prayer. It is effectual prayer, earnest prayer, with sweat. Explicit, enduring and God-exalting. That kind of prayer prevails before the throne of God. That is what Wesley said, "Storm the throne of grace and the blessings and the power will come down as a result of you and me continuing to come before the throne of God, pleading." That is why God said, "Come boldly to the throne of grace."

We need to prevail in prayer. We are never going to have revival without prevailing prayer. It is the primary element in genuine revival. Getting right with God, and then saturating your whole town and your life and your church and everything with prayer, the kind of prayer we talked about, prevailing prayer. The answer will come if it is prevailing prayer. It will be honored by God Almighty. He said, *"The effectual fervent prayer of a of a righteous man availeth much."* In the healing of a body, in the salvation of a soul, in promoting a revival, you name it, *"The effectual fervent prayer of a righteous man availeth much"* in every instance.   It always does.

I wonder how many effectual fervent prayers of a righteous man have gone up today from you.   I wonder how many of us have prayed like we are instructed to today.   We have to take the prayer closet more seriously, and the prayer meeting more seriously.   It is the power-house of God and the powerhouse of every church.   Prayer moves the hand of God, and you and I need to prevail in prayer.   Pray until the answer comes.   Do not give up.   Do not give in.   Prevailing prayer.

CHAPTER NINE

THE WEAPON OF PRAYER

"For though we walk in the flesh, we do not war after the flesh: (For the weapons of our warfare are not carnal, but mighty through God to the pulling down of strong holds;) Casting down imaginations, and every high thing that exalteth itself against the knowledge of God, and bringing into captivity every thought to the obedience of Christ." (II Corinthians 10:3-5)

Notice several things about the text that Paul stated. He said we are in fleshly bodies, but our warfare is not a fleshly warfare. That tells me that I am at war, not at peace. There are a lot of folks that do not realize that and so they get wounded because they are not being sober and vigilant. When people get to walking around unaware in the middle of a battle zone, they are about to get wounded.

You will be a casualty if you do not realize that you are at war. Regardless of what goes on in the Middle East or South Africa, if they establish peace we are at war, and it is a spiritual warfare. It has been waged through the centuries between the emissaries of Satan and the servants of God. Realize that we are at war.

Paul said, *"Be sober, be vigilant, because your adversary the devil, as a roaring lion, walketh about, seeking whom he may devour."* He devours lives. If the devil has his way, he will sift everything good out of you and throw the shell to the wind. There will not be anything left that is worthwhile.

Sometimes the devil can wound us through our own poor perception. The year I graduated from Bible college we had a fella who was a janitor. He was a fine man, but it bothered him that he had never finished high school. The faculty, unaware of this, decided that they were going to do something to recognize him for his hard work. They wanted it to be a surprise. They had heard about a janitor who had been given a certificate that said "Doctor of Custodiology". At graduation they planned to bring him down to the front and put the cap and gown on him to honor him before the people for his faithful service. Everybody gave him a standing ovation.

As soon as the graduation ceremony was over he went to the preacher's office, threw his keys on the desk, and said, "I quit." He was offended. He thought they were trying to make fun of his lack of schooling, when they were actually trying to let him know how much they appreciated his faithfulness and hard work. He got wounded by the devil because of poor perception.

Do not be shocked if you get wounded. "I quit! I tried to serve the Lord, but I got wounded." What did you expect in a war? Do you think the enemy is not going to shoot back? Do you think nobody is ever going to get hurt? Do you think there will never be a casualty? Certainly there will be. But God has given me enough protection to keep from being a fatality. Even if I get wounded, it does not have to destroy me completely.

When Paul speaks of being sober and vigilant that is the way you would walk through a mine field. Be on the lookout all the time. Do not be careless. You are not haphazard or relaxed if you are in a mine field. You are on guard, looking, carefully watching where you tread, making every move count, being careful what you do. That is how we are supposed to live in awareness of the enemy.

The second thing I want you to notice is that this is not a carnal warfare, but a spiritual warfare. In

Ephesians 6:12 the Bible says, *"For we wrestle not against flesh and blood, but against principalities, against powers, against the rulers of the darkness of this world, against spiritual wickedness in high places."* Our warfare is not with other men, it is on a spiritual plane. We get distracted by men a lot of times, but there is a devil and the demons of hell behind every attack that man launches. That man is nothing more than a pawn in the game. The devil is moving the pieces.

If I am going to have success in this warfare, I must have an impact on the one moving the pieces, not just the pieces. We get so preoccupied and distracted by what men do, so caught up in skirmishes with men that we never fight the true battle. That is exactly what the devil would like for us to do. We fail to recognize that our warfare is not a carnal warfare with men, but a spiritual warfare with the devil himself.

Several years ago I was in Jacksonville, Florida, holding a revival meeting. On Saturday morning out soulwinning, I got out into the hot sun and started breaking out in poison ivy all over my body. Somehow it got it into my system and every time a sweat bead would pop out, poison ivy would come out there. I was in misery. After about an hour I told the preacher, "I have to go and get something done about this."

I went down to the local drug store and was told that I could not get anything strong without a prescription. I said, "What do you have?" They said, "We have some Calamine lotion. It will help to ease the itching." But it does not cure the problem. I wanted some relief so I got the lotion and painted myself with about five gallons of it. It eased the itch, for a short while. But soon it started itching again and I still was not cured of the problem.

I finally called my office and told them to get a hold of my doctor and tell him that I needed a prescription down in Florida for some Cortisone and Benadryl. The doctor's office called down and got it all set up. When I took the right medicine, it cured me from the inside. In the meantime, I kept the Calamine lotion on the outside. There was nothing wrong with trying to make the symptoms less painful. It just never would have taken care of the problem alone.

Before my dad had a heart attack, he had pain down his left arm. As long as we rubbed his arm and gave it constant attention it eased the pain, but as soon as we quit rubbing the arm it would return. Then he went to the doctor and got medicine for his heart. Strange thing. When he got the medicine for his heart the pain in his arm went away. The pain in his arm was not the problem. It was a symptom of the real problem. If you spend all of your time on the symptom, you will never cure the problem.

Our battle is not with men. We get so wound up when bad legislation is going to be passed. "Shouldn't you do something about it?" Yes, I think we should. But for every hour I spend fighting bad legislation I had better spend two hours in the prayer closet fighting the devil who is using somebody to pass it. We get preoccupied with the symptoms. We get bitter against people in the battle and destroy our testimonies and ruin our spirit, and never realize what the devil is doing to us. This warfare is a spiritual warfare. If we are ever going to make a real difference, we are going to have to fight it on a spiritual plane.

Notice in verse four, our weapons are mighty, not weak. To hear some preachers, you would really think that nothing could be done about the evils of society and the ungodliness that is going on. "Well, we are in the last days. There is going to be a great apostacy." The last days started in the Book of Acts. They did not start yesterday. We can make all the excuses that we want to for being sorry. But if we would learn how to pray and do what we ought to do in the areas of prayer and soul-winning, we could make some changes instead making excuses.

God said 'weapons' --- not singular but plural. Not just weapons in general, but mighty weapons. We do not have to roll over and play dead. We do not have to get into a defensive mode. We have all the power of heaven available to make a spiritual attack. Anything God provides is not weak. The weakness of God is stronger than men. These mighty, powerful, spiritual weapons are available to us as God's children for the battles that we face.

Verse four in our text speaks of weapons, not shields. It does not say, "Our shields are heavy duty." No, the emphasis is on weapons for offensive warfare. The indication here is that I am to be on the attack. You are no match for the devil. If you let him shoot first every time you are not going to win. If he gets the first punch in, you are going to get the stuffings beat out of you. If you are in a defensive mode, reacting instead of acting, you are not going to defeat him. You have to launch the attack and get on the offense. We have weapons, not shields.

In Ephesians chapter six the Bible tells me about my armor. In verse thirteen it says, *"Wherefore take unto you the whole armour of God, that ye may be able to withstand in the evil day, and having done all, to stand."* If you do not get equipped with God's armor, you will not be able to stand.

Notice this first piece of armor mentioned. *"Stand therefore, having your loins girt about with truth."* The girdle of truth. Now, I believe that I am protected from becoming a fatality by the truth of God's Word, and by Jesus Who is the Way, the Truth, and the Life. But I

think there is more to it than that. Truth and honesty in
my daily Christian life will be a protection for me from
the onslaught of the devil.

Notice what part of my life is protected -- the loins,
the midsection of the body. I believe that is talking about
my morality. People that slip around and sneak around
and are crooked, who are always trying to do something
and then lie about it will be immoral because they have
an immoral mind. Truth protects the loins. Truth
protects you morally.

We have trouble with that. A lot of people who could
have done great things for God, who had great potential
and in past times did great things for God did not use
truth as a protection for them. They were too sneaky and
slithery. You will not get by with that.

*"And having on the breastplate of right-
eousness."* The gladiators taught that a wound in the
chest cavity was a mortal wound, a fatal wound. The
breastplate protects that area where the heart is.

The breastplate of righteousness, or 'right living,' will
keep me from getting a mortal wound that will destroy
me totally. When Paul talks about righteousness here he
is not just talking about salvation and imputed righteousness. He is talking about personal, practical
righteousness; living the right kind of life, doing the right
thing.

Just doing right is a protection. Your habits ought to
be habits of doing right. Your schedule ought to revolve
around doing right, doing the will of God. Even when you
are not in perfect condition spiritually, your righteousness, or right living and habits of doing right, will
help to protect you from destruction.

In verse fifteen he talks about your feet being shod
with the preparation of the Gospel of peace. Soulwinning
will protect you. If I am in the will of God there is

protection there. When I stray out of His will then I lose the protection that is provided. God has prescribed for me where I am to go, what I am to do, and I am protected by the Gospel of peace, by being a soulwinner.

If David had been where he was supposed to be when he was supposed to be there, he would have never seen Bathsheba. It was time for kings to go forth to war, but David abode at home. It was time for soulwinners to go forth soulwinning, and some Christian was being lax and lazy, and it led him into sin. They were good, sincere Christian people, but they saw something they should not have seen, they did something they should not have done, and they wrecked themselves. The enemy defeated them.

Soulwinning protects my feet from the rough and rocky road. My soulwinning shoes help me to bear the weight of the burden, and to complete the entire journey. Soulwinning protects my feet by keeping them on the right path.

"Above all, taking the shield of faith." Everything in the Christian life has to be seasoned and salted with faith. Faith is not a passive word. It says, "By faith Noah imagined an ark," right? Oh, he built one? So faith must mean movement, activity. Faith always indicates doing. Faith is when the Word of God is enough. I do not need a tingle. I do not need a sign. I do not need a miracle. If God said it that is good enough. I will do it because He said so. That is faith. That is all Noah had. He had never seen a flood, or even a rain shower. He had to go strictly by the Word of God. I am supposed to operate by faith, too.

"Take the helmet of salvation." The helmet protects my mind. I believe the helmet of salvation is having a saved mind as well as a saved soul. Many people have been born again and their names are written down in heaven, but they think and act and react just like the

unsaved world. My mind ought to be saturated with the Word of God, so that I can operate with the mind of Christ.

"...and the sword of the Spirit." So far, we have been talking about defenses, armor to shield us from the attacks of our enemy. Did you notice, God did not give us anything for the back of the coward? I am supposed to go forward. Now we come to the sword. The sword is our offensive weapon. It is for me to make attack, to take the battle to the devil. I have the *"sword of the Spirit, which is the word of God."* Wait a minute. The Word of God does not go anywhere by itself. Someone has to carry it. That is conventional warfare. That is man-to-man combat. I take the Word of God and fight the devil one sinner at a time, winning them one at a time with the Word of God. I have to go in physically to do that. I must fight the battle one on one to do that. What a powerful weapon.

Then he identifies our second mighty weapon. *"Praying always with all prayer and supplication in the Spirit, and watching thereunto with all perseverance and supplication for all saints."* The second weapon I have is the weapon of prayer. Now we are moving from conventional weapons to nuclear power. That is my air attack. I can cover a lot more ground in my prayer closet than I can on foot. I can only affect one person at a time, on the spot, with the Bible. That is a very necessary part of my battle plan. But it is the large scale attack that is going to make the greatest impact. Prayer is my nuclear weapon, with which I can have an effect on great masses of people and places where I will never be.

Prayer is for attack, a mighty spiritual weapon. It is not just for getting things from God, although God wants me to do that, too. The honest truth is, the average person does not pray much at all. But those of us who pray, pray about ten minutes when we need something really bad. Most of us have never once, in our entire lives, launched an attack on the devil in prayer. I would dare say that we never use prayer as an offensive weapon to pull down the strong holds and break down his barriers and loose those he has captivated.

We are to be on offense, not on defense. In Matthew 16:18 Jesus said, *"...upon this rock I will build my church; and the gates of hell shall not prevail against it."* Somebody gets up and says, "Bless God, the Bible says the gates of hell shall not prevail against the church. The devil cannot destroy the church." That is true, but you miss the whole point. A gate is not a weapon. He is not talking about the devil getting the gate out and attacking the church with it. A gate is a strong hold, for protection. A gate is to keep something secure. "The gates of hell shall not prevail against the church." He is not talking about the devil getting the gate after the church. He is talking about the church launching a spiritual attack against the gates of hell, and the forces of hell cannot prevail against a Spirit-filled, praying church that is using God's weapons in this spiritual warfare.

When He speaks of the "gates of hell" here He is not talking about the lake of fire. He is talking about the forces of hell and the strong holds of the devil that have people captivated by the devil. Hebrews chapter two says there are some people the devil takes at will. They are captives. They are in his family. They belong to him. The gates of hell are the strongholds that keep people captive under the dominion of Satan.

In the Bible, the gate was also a seat of judgment. The city fathers used to sit at the gate and give counsel and wisdom and pass down decisions for the people. All the wisdom and counsel of this world's system and the god of this world cannot prevail against a sin-fighting, prayer-saturated, soulwinning church.

The gate was a fortification or a strong hold. It was for security or protection. It was to keep others out. But the gates of hell shall not prevail against the church. That means that a Spirit-filled, soulwinning church cannot be stopped by the devil. He cannot prevent us from loosing sinners from the bondage of their sin and bringing them to liberty in Christ.

In the next verse, Matthew 16:19, Jesus said, *"I will give unto thee the keys of the kingdom of heaven: and whatsoever thou shalt bind on earth shall be bound in heaven: and whatsoever thou shalt loose on earth shall be loosed in heaven."* He is giving us keys. Keys indicate authority. If a guy has some keys he has some responsibility, some authority, some access where others are locked out.

Keys are to unlock things. Jesus said we have the keys to the kingdom. God has all the power that is needed. I have the key that unlocks it. So why am I doing without? There is a power available to the child of God that the devil cannot match. The power available to me is the kingdom of light. Light always drives back darkness. Darkness will never prevail against light, it always flees away. The Bible says that I have the key to unlock that power of God, that authority of God, to launch an attack on the devil and to win.

The problem is this: We are trying to fight a spiritual war with carnal weapons. That is about like trying to fight a tank with a bb gun -- then you wonder why you have half track marks on your forehead. You are sitting there plinking at an armored tank with a bb gun while you have a rocket launcher at your fingertips, and refuse to use it. Not too smart.

Paul said, *"Pulling down strong holds."* The gate was the entrance way to a strong hold where the devil has captives. A prison camp, if you please. He has captivated people and he has their lives chained up in the strong hold of alcohol, and the strong hold of drugs, and the strong hold of homosexuality and every kind of sexual perversion, the strong hold of pornography. The devil has captivated people. They are bound up in sin; slaves to it. They cannot seem to do anything on their own. Someone is going to have to come to their rescue. God has given us access to the power that can do it.

How do we pull down the strong holds? In Matthew 18:18 Jesus almost duplicates Matthew 16:19. It is almost word-for-word. *"Verily I say unto you, Whatsoever ye shall bind on earth shall be bound in heaven: and whatsoever ye shall loose on earth shall be loosed in heaven."* We heard that statement twice. How do you bind anything? How do you loose anything? Let's read on. *"Again I say unto you, That if two of you shall agree on earth as touching any thing that they shall ask, it shall be done for them of my Father which is in heaven."* Dr. Rice said prayer is asking and receiving.

How do I bind something? Ask. How do I loose something? Ask. Pray. The weapon of prayer. He said, "Whatever you ask it shall be done unto you of my Father." Notice, *"If two of you shall agree."* That is the word for symphonize, or harmonize. If you have an organ and a piano and you want to get them in tune you do not take the tuning fork and tune the piano and then put the tuning fork away and try to get the organ in tune with the piano. You take the tuning fork and tune the piano. You take the exact same tuning fork and tune the organ. When they are in tune with the same tuning fork, they are automatically in tune with each other.

It is not my job to adjust to everybody else. It is my job to adjust to the Holy Spirit. It is not your job to adjust to everybody else. It is your job to adjust to the Holy Spirit. If I am in tune with Him, and you are in tune with Him we will be in tune with each other. There will be symphony and harmony and unity and power in prayer. We can launch a spiritual attack and have an impact on the devil.

Matthew 18:20 is a verse that is often misused. It says, *"For where two or three are gathered together in my name, there am I in the midst of them."* It does not say, "Where two or three are gathered together, there is a church." Some folks say, "Well, I don't go to church, but where two or three are gathered there am I in the midst." There is a lot more to a church than just two or three people gathered together. If there is a God-called pastor sent out to do the work for the glory of God it could be a church. But just a bunch of folks coming together in rebellion against the Word of God does not make it a church, whether you have three or three thousand.

This is a prayer promise. Do not let people pull it out of context. Jesus said, "If you will get in tune with Me and the Spirit of God and come together in prayer, I will be in the midst."

There are definite illustrations of binding and loosing in the Bible. You remember in Acts chapter twelve the Bible tells us that James had been killed with the sword and Peter had been put into jail. He was scheduled to be executed. The church came together and prayed. As they prayed God sent an angel and loosed Peter. Isn't it amazing? He put a deep sleep on all sixteen of those soldiers, the cuffs fell off Peter's hands, the iron door opened, the gate opened and he walked out into the street led by the angel. If those Christians in the early church had tried to accomplish that conventionally there would have been some bloodshed.

But they decided to go ahead and put an air attack on. They got the nuclear weapons out. They prayed and the angel did what they could not do. The angel loosed him out of the prison in answer to prayer.

The Bible talks about binding. There was a man by the name of Hosea in the Old Testament whose wife went off into harlotry. The Bible says that Hosea prayed a hedge of thorns about her and made her unsavory in the eyes of her lovers. His prayer life prevented her from doing what she wanted to do. That is called binding.

In Matthew 12:28 Jesus said, *"But if I cast out devils by the Spirit of God, then the kingdom of God is come unto you. Or else how can one enter into a strong man's house, and spoil his goods, except he first bind the strong man? and then he will spoil his house."* Who is the strong man? The devil. Jesus said you first have to bind the strong man, then you can enter into his house and spoil his goods. What is the most precious thing in your house? Children? Family members?

In John 8:44 Jesus said, *"Ye are of your father the devil."* He said anybody outside of Jesus Christ was a child of the devil. They are in his family. If I am going to enter his house and spoil his goods the first thing I have to do is bind that strong man in prayer. Then I can walk in and get sinners out of there. When the devil is loosed, I cannot get in and the sinner cannot get out. But once I bind the the devil through prayer, then I can enter in and get the job done.

I am weary of people who say, "Well, this is a hard area." Every area is a hard area until somebody softens it with prayer. Somebody has to pay the price in the prayer closet. Somebody has to launch a nuclear attack, an air attack to get the job done. Every area is a strong hold of Satan until somebody breaks down the bars. What we are trying to do is spoil his goods without binding the strong man. We are trying to win the city without softening it by prayer. We are trying to do it strictly with conventional weapons, and we are making it hard on ourselves when it could be much easier.

Remember what happened in Vietnam? We had the power to win that war over night. But instead we fought a bloody battle that costs thousands of lives and much grief. I believe we are having all kinds of casualties and little results even though we have the power to win, because our weapons are back there gathering dust in the back room somewhere. We are not using the weapons that God has made available.

Remember the war in Iraq? American troops went in there and camped on the border. Hussein had his best troops on the border. He threatened a bloody ground war. So we carpet bombed, and carpet bombed, and carpet bombed, and carpet bombed, and launched missiles off of the ships, and shelled it from the big guns. We broke down their strongholds and weakened their forces. Then, almost without resistance, we went in and took over.

You cannot take a strategic position without going in with ground troops, and prayer is never going to replace soulwinning. Air attack can never replace the work of the ground troops, it just paves the way and makes it easier. The carpet bombing softened the resistance. They had broken down the strong holds and bound the strong man and ran that little weasel into a hole. They accomplished it with an air attack, then they came in and took the positions with ease.

Prayer is my carpet bombing, my air attack. I am supposed to get on my face before God and launch the weapon of prayer and carpet bomb, and carpet bomb, and carpet bomb, and then I can spoil his goods and free the children that he has held captive all that time.

Even while our ground troops went in, they did not stop the air attack. You do not quit praying to go soulwinning. You keep praying while you are soulwinning. Go ahead and soften the territory, then you go, and while you go you get some air support. Let God continue to soften some things. Jesus prayed all night. He was carpet bombing. Then in the daytime he saved people by the thousands. If the Son of God needed to spend that much time in launching that great weapon of prayer, softening the territory, how much more do frail beings like you and me need to do it?

Paul prayed continually in every epistle he wrote. He talked about his prayer life for others. He was always launching an air attack. But then he loosed people from their sin and he had an effect on people's lives. He saw thousands of people saved.

The early church locked themselves in a room, one hundred and twenty of them. They prayed for ten days, pouring out their souls. It says they were all in one place in one accord. What was that passage in Matthew chapter eighteen? If we would what? Agree. Everybody was not out to see what they could get and to see if they could be somebody famous. They came together with one mind, one heart, one soul, in unity, in agreement with the Holy Spirit. It produced agreement with each other. They spent ten days carpet bombing. When they came out of that room three thousand people got saved and three thousand people got baptized in one day in the hardest city on the face of the earth, Jerusalem.

There is no harder city than Jerusalem. I believe it is the hardest city still today. The disciples had an impact because they honored the principle of using the weapon of prayer to soften the defenses, and then using the Word of God, loosed one sinner at a time. We are out there with the Word of God, and thank God for it, but we are not getting done what we could get done if we would learn to launch the weapon of prayer.

In Acts 19:13-16 you find the story of the seven sons of Sceva. They had some contact with Paul. They had seen him pray and perform miracles. They had seen him cast out devils in the power of the Holy Spirit by calling on the name of Jesus. Paul prayed with mighty power and there was an impact. These seven sons of Sceva were vagabonds and exorcists. Let me help you with something. Exorcism has never been a Christian practice. Jesus Christ never did one exorcism. He did deliver people from the power of Satan. But exorcism has always been an occult practice. Exorcism is when you get the demon out of somebody else into yourself. Buddy, if you have demons, you keep them. Do not be dabbling with occult practices, it will destroy you.

There is such a thing as the power of God delivering somebody from those demons. They are real. So here were these seven sons of Sceva. They came to a demon possessed guy and said, "In the name of Jesus, whom Paul preacheth, we command you to come out of him." The fella jumped up and beat the fire out of them, tore their clothes off and ran them out of the house. Before that he said, *"Jesus I know, and Paul I know; but who are ye?"* He said, "What do you mean, trying to hinder me? You do not have any power. You have never slowed my work down before. I have had trouble with Jesus. He has tied me in a knot. I have had trouble with Paul breaking down the strong holds. But who are you?"

I am afraid the devil might ask any one of us the same thing. We have so little power with God and we know so little about prayer and we spend so little time in waging a spiritual warfare.

Jesus and Paul were known by those demons of hell

because of their prayer lives and the mighty spiritual power that they exuded. Both were soulwinners. To be quite frank with you, I do not believe you can get your prayers answered if you are not a soulwinner. John 15:16 says, *"Ye have not chosen me, but I have chosen you, and ordained you, that ye should go and bring forth fruit, and that your fruit should remain: that whatsoever ye shall ask of the Father in my name, he may give it you."* That means if I do not win souls, if I do not bear fruit, He has prohibited Himself, He may not do that because of His holiness. He may not answer my prayer if I am not bearing fruit. I give God the opportunity to answer my prayer if I am a soulwinner. You are not going to be much of a danger to the devil if you are not a soulwinner to start with.

Evan Roberts headed the great Welsh Revival many years ago that literally exterminated sin. One secular reporter from the United States who visited there in the midst of the revival said, "I could not find a trace of the devil. There were no arrests for months. Bar rooms closed down. Places of ill repute went out of business. Places of entertainment closed down for lack of a crowd. Churches were filled to capacity. Tens of thousands of people were saved." Do you know how it all started? One teenage girl who believed God would answer prayer began to pray. Then some other folks decided to pray. It was not built on preaching as much as on praying.

They came to a place during their lunch hour every day and they prayed. The next day they brought someone with them and they prayed. After lunch they would go out and lead people to Christ. The next day they would bring their converts to the prayer meeting. Before you knew it they could not get them all into the building. They went into a bigger building and filled that up. Every day they came together, and prayed and begged

God for His power, and God moved across the face of that land in a mighty way.

If you and I do not get back to the weapon of prayer we are going to get run over by the devil. I am for soul-winning as much as anybody in America. I believe in it. I practice it. I go virtually every day of my life. But if we do not get back to the weapon of prayer, if we do not learn to launch an air attack, we are making something that could be so easy so hard.

The weapon of prayer. You ought to decide today that you are going to get this powerful weapon out and begin to use it. You have the key to unlock the power of God. If we are going to have anything that resembles the early church we must not only have the doctrine of the early church and the separation of the early church, we must have the prayer life of the early church.

Even most people who pray on a consistent basis have never used prayer as an offensive weapon to attack the devil. Prayer is the means of getting things from God. I do not want to take that aspect of prayer away. Thank God that He hears and answers and gives us what we ask for. But it is also a powerful weapon to bind the strong man and to loose his captives and spoil his goods. We are not using it that way. God help us today to get the weapon of prayer out and dust it off, and launch an air attack that will make our conventional warfare ten times easier and more productive. The weapon of prayer. A neglected, ignored, powerful weapon. You need not be afraid of the weapon of prayer. It is our nuclear power but it never damages anything good. It only unleashes the mighty power of the wonderful God in heaven. Do not be afraid to unleash that power in the prayer closet. The weapon of prayer.

CHAPTER TEN

HOLY HEDGES

"Then Satan answered the LORD, and said, Doth Job fear God for nought? Hast thou not made an hedge about him, and about his house, and about all that he hath on every side? thou hast blessed the work of his hands, and his substance is increased in the land. But put forth thine hand now, and touch all that he hath, and he will curse thee to thy face." (Job 1:9-11)

The devil was complaining to God. Job chapter one says, *"There was a man in the land of Uz, whose name was Job; and that man was perfect and upright, and one that feared God and eschewed evil."* It talks about how many sons he had and all that God had placed in his hands, all of his material possessions, all of his wealth. It was the blessing of God. God had given him everything that he had.

There was a time when the sons of God came before God in heaven and Satan was also among them. God said to the devil, "Have you considered my servant Job that there is none like him in all the earth? He is the best Christian alive. There is nobody like Job." The devil made an accusation in verses nine, ten and eleven. He said, "Doth Job serve You for nought? Anybody would serve You if You put a hedge around them and protected them. You have a hedge about everything that he has, all of his possessions, himself, his family. He has good health. He has wealth. He has prosperity. His family is alive and well, no hardship, no problems. You have a hedge around him. Why shouldn't he serve You?"

Then the devil said, "If You would take that hedge

away and let me attack Job, he will curse You." This is the accusation that the devil is making. He said, "Job does not serve You for who You are. He serves You for what You do." The tragedy is that for so many of us that is true. The proof of that is that when things go sour for us we turn bitter on God. We make accusations against God. In the time we need Him the most and should flee to His presence we turn from Him and get out of church. What is that? That is bitterness. You do not think God is worthy of worship unless He does what you like, right?

God had literally put a hedge about Job. A hedge separates us. It cuts us off from another area. It divides things. It is a line of demarcation, a boundary, a property line. A hedge also confines us. It keeps us in a certain area. It keeps us within certain boundaries. But inside those boundaries there is safety. Inside those boundaries there is protection. Inside those boundaries there is blessing. A hedge protects from certain things. A hedge can, and sometimes does, identify. In our case it certainly does.

There are two kinds of hedges in Scripture. The first one is a hedge of separation. When the Bible speaks of separation, it is not just separating from something, it is separating unto something and Someone. I am not just separated from sin and the devil and worldliness, I am separated unto God and holiness and righteousness. I am not just separated from evil works, I am separated unto good works. In Psalm 37:27 the Bible says, *"Depart from evil, and do good; and dwell forever more."*

The Bible tells us to *"...come out from among them, and be ye separate, saith the Lord; and touch not the unclean thing."* That means there is a wrong crowd. That means there are things that I am to separate from.

The hedge of separation is seen in the life of Job.

When God described Job in verse eight, He said unto Satan, *"Hast thou considered my servant Job, that there is none like him in the earth, a perfect and an upright man, one that feareth God and escheweth evil?"* Everybody who is saved does not automatically have a hedge of protection against the devil. I cannot lose my salvation. I cannot lose my eternal soul. I believe that God gives me a certain amount of hedging and protection when I get saved, but if I do not separate I will break that hedge down and I will give the devil place in my life. I will give him room to wreck my life.

The devil did not complain about the whole human race having a hedge about them, did he? He did not complain that every saved person on the face of the earth had a hedge about them, did he? His complaint was that this fellow, Job, had a hedge about him and the devil could not touch him without permission.

The Bible says Job was God's servant. He was not here to fulfill his lustful desires. He was here to serve a God who is a Spirit. He had given himself to God, lock, stock and barrel.

Job was a peculiar fellow. The Bible says in the Book of Titus, chapter two that we are supposed to be a peculiar people. We are to be zealous of good works. Job was not the generic, run-of-the-mill, so-called born again believer. There was something different about him. I imagine to the general public he was somewhat of an oddball. He was a little strange. He did not indulge in carnality like the average saved person does.

God also said he was perfect. The word 'perfect' in the Scripture, when it speaks of man, is not speaking of sinlessness. It means mature, complete. It is talking about fulness of stature. It is talking about being Christ-like.

But that is not all. The Bible says Job was upright. The thought indicated here is the integrity of his heart. He was not only upright outwardly (there are a lot of hypocrites who do the right kinds of things), he did not just look good on the outside; he was upright in his heart. He had pure motives in his heart. He had a love for God in his heart. His heart was clean. His motive was pure. His desire was right. He was a man of honesty and integrity. He was genuine. He was real.

Job feared God. When the Bible speaks of the fear of the Lord, it does not mean I stand and quake and fear God, like He is a mean bully. Job had a reverence for God that caused him to live like he ought to live. In other words, a person who fears God is a person who lives every moment of every hour of every day in light of the judgment seat of Christ. That is what the fear of the Lord is; living with the reality that God is watching me right now.

I feared my dad, but only when I had done wrong. We were very close. But I had a fear, and a reverence, and a respect for him. I only had to exercise fear when I had disobeyed him.

The Bible says Job eschewed evil. That means he had an intense hatred for evil. It means he had the same attitude towards sin that God has towards it. Did you know that God hates sin? The Bible says in Psalm 97:10, ***"Ye that love the Lord, hate evil."*** Job hated the sin that corrupted man and ruined his life.

If I am to have the kind of protection Job had, if I am to be the kind of Christian Job was, I need to be a servant of God. I need to be a peculiar person. I need to be mature and maturing. I need to be upright and have integrity in my heart. I need to have a fear of the Lord and I need to have an intense hatred for evil. When I do those things, I can experience that hedge of protection. God knows, every one of us needs His protection. The devil walks about as a roaring lion, seeking whom he may devour. But he cannot come inside the hedge. If I were you, I would not leave the gate open. If I were you, I would not knock a hole in the hedge with sin and rebellion and self will.

I would realize that though I am saved and the devil cannot take my salvation from me, he can certainly wreck my life. Though he cannot send me to an eternal hell, he can help me to create a little bit of a hell on earth for myself and my family. He can bring a lot of heartache and tragedy and sorrow into my life if I do not put myself into a position where God can hedge me about.

Let me remind you that Job was the only one the devil complained about having this kind of a hedge of separation about him. There were other saved people in the world, but the devil had mastery over them and had wrecked their lives. He was not too concerned about them. He had an avenue to attack them any time he wanted and cause havoc in their lives. This fellow Job irritated the devil. He could not touch him. He had separated himself unto God to such a degree that God had him hedged about.

In Ephesians 6:10-18, God talks about putting on the armor; the breastplate of righteousness, the loins girt about with truth, the feet shod with the preparation of the Gospel. Paul described many of the attributes and character traits in Ephesians six that were in the life of Job. God said He had provided armor. Job had it on. Job had applied the principles in the Book to his life.

In Isaiah chapter thirty-five the Bible gives us a millennial promise. It talks about the provision and the protection of God. But I believe there is an application for our day. In verses eight through ten He talks about the way of holiness. He said, *"The unclean shall not pass over it."* If I walk in the path of holiness, I will walk with God. God will not leave the path of holiness to walk with me, but if I will enter the path of holiness He is waiting for me to walk with Him. I do not have to worry about the unclean, the wicked, the defiled, or the ungodly mixing with me and confusing me. They will not pass over the way of holiness.

"Fools...shall not err therein." The fool does not want to be there. There are a lot of the characteristics of the fool in the Book of Proverbs. He is brutish. He will not take advice. He has a hot temper. God says I do not have to worry about being influenced by these kinds of people if I am in the way of holiness.

"No lion shall be there." In I Peter 5:8 the Bible says, *"Be sober, be vigilant, because your adversary, the devil, as a roaring lion, walketh about, seeking whom he may devour."* He cannot get into the way of holiness. It is hedged up. The fool will not make it through the hedge. It takes too much effort, anyway. The unclean will not pass through there. The lion, the beast, and the devil will not be there.

"Nor any ravenous beast." The devil and all the forces of hell cannot enter into that area. The beasts, the demonic creatures that are under his dominion cannot get in. I am protected in the way of holiness. In Proverbs 16:17 the Bible says, *"The highway of the upright is to depart from evil: he that keepeth his way preserveth his soul."* I will preserve my soul, and the joy and peace and contentment of my soul by getting in the way of holiness. I do not have to worry about trying to create a hedge. If I will separate myself unto God and walk in the way of holiness, it is hedged up already. The devil cannot touch me without permission.

A lot of us have knocked so many holes in the hedge that the devil can do just about anything he wants to with us. We have erred outside of the way of holiness.

We have not separated ourselves unto God. We are not servants of God. We are immature spiritually. We are allowing all kinds of other things to manipulate us. We are free game for the devil and the demons of hell to attack us.

The hedge of separation is available to any child of God who will separate himself and be clean and holy like Job and walk in the way of holiness. God wants it for everybody. But if you would rather fight with beasts everyday, so that you can have your own way instead of God's way, you can knock the hedge out. You can get outside the hedge. You can wander wherever you like, but you will face constant attacks and you will not win.

There is another hedge in Scripture, the hedge of supplication. This is not a hedge that I obtain by doing something as far as separation or cleanness. This is a hedge that I provide for someone else in the prayer closet. In Ezekiel 22:30, God said, *"I sought for a man among them, that should make up the hedge, and stand in the gap before me for the land, that I should not destroy it: but I found none."* Did you notice, I am not standing to represent God to the people, I am standing before God to represent somebody else.

The hedge of supplication that I can provide for someone else in the prayer closet protects them from the judgment of God. I am pleading their case. I am paying a price. I am standing in the gap. I am making up a hedge of prayer to protect them.

This is illustrated numbers of times in the Bible. You remember the prophet by the name of Hosea who had a harlot for a wife. The Bible says that Hosea prayed and God put a hedge of thorns around Gomer and made her unsavory in the eyes of her lovers. It was Hosea's intercessory prayer that did this.

The word 'supplication' means to pray with sweat.

If you are going to supplicate you may have to come in the middle of the night. Jesus told of the man who came at midnight, knocking on someone's door. He said, "I have a friend who has come to my house and I have nothing to set before him." He was answered, "Go away. We are in bed." He said, "You do not understand." He did not come for bread for himself. He came at midnight for bread for somebody else, for a traveller on a journey to eternity. I have nothing to give them unless I come before God and get the bread to take back and give to them.

In Exodus 32:9-14 the people of Israel had angered God. He said, "Okay, Moses, get away from them. I am going to kill the whole bunch of them. I will start over with you and your family. I have had it with them." Moses fell on his face and began to weep. He said, "Oh, God. The Egyptians will see that You brought the people out here to kill them in the wilderness and they will say You did not have the power to deliver them." He was supplicating. He was begging God and pleading their case and reasoning with God. He said, "Lord, if You are going to do it, just go ahead and blot me out of the book, too. Just go ahead and kill me with them." God withheld His hand of judgment. Moses provided a hedge of supplication.

In Luke 22:31-32 Jesus told Peter, *"Satan hath desired to have you, that he may sift you as wheat; But I have prayed for thee, that thy faith fail not."* Peter went on to deny the Lord, but the devil did not sift him as wheat. When you sift wheat you crack the shell, get the wheat out of it, drain all that is good until there is nothing left but an empty shell and you cast it to the wind. That is what the devil wants to do with every Christian's life. He wants to squeeze anything that is good out of you and then throw the empty shell to the wind.

Peter did not have the hedge of separation, but he had the hedge of supplication. Someone else supplicated for him when he was unseparated and salvaged him from sure and total wreckage. I am glad Jesus is interceding for me because He always gets His prayers answered.

We have seen two kinds of hedges. The hedge of separation is provided for everybody that will be the kind of Christian that Job was; separated. Then there is the hedge of supplication that the separated Christian can pray about somebody else; his loved ones, his family, his possessions, his church, his pastor, his community, his nation.

Sometimes the hedges are removed. There are only two times when I see the hedge of separation removed. The first of those I want to show you in Isaiah chapter five. One reason the hedge is removed is because wild grapes are brought forth. *'Now will I sing to my well beloved a song of my beloved touching his vineyard. My well beloved hath a vineyard in a very fruitful hill: And he fenced it, and gathered out the stones thereof, and planted it with the choicest vine, and built a tower in the midst of it, and also made a winepress therein: and he looked that it should bring forth grapes, and it brought forth wild grapes. And now, O inhabitants of Jerusalem, and men of Judah, judge, I pray you, betwixt me and my vineyard. What could have been done more to my vineyard, that I have not done in it? wherefore, when I looked that it should bring forth grapes, brought it forth wild grapes? And now go to; I will tell you what I will do to my vineyard: I will take away the hedge thereof, and it shall be eaten up; and break down the wall thereof, and it shall be trodden down: And I will lay it waste: it shall not be pruned, nor digged; but there shall come up briers and thorns: I will also command the clouds that they rain no rain upon it."*

God will remove the hedge when I refuse to bring forth the fruit of righteousness. It is not a matter of ignorance, of me not knowing any better. It is not a matter of me being too weak, of being a baby Christian. It is a matter of me being saved for years and being a carnal Christian. There is a difference between a baby Christian and a carnal Christian. A carnal Christian is one who is old enough to be a teacher.

In Hebrews 5:12 the Bible says, *"For when for the time ye ought to be teachers, ye have need that one teach you again which be the first principles of the oracles of God; and are become such as have need of milk, and not of strong meat."* God said He would take away the hedge when I bring forth wild grapes. That is when I err outside the way of holiness. That is when I refuse to respond to the leading and the pleading of God. That is when God has saved me and put a hedge about me and protected me, He has nurtured me, He has watered me, He has pruned me, then, in rebellion, I bring forth wild grapes because I do not appreciate all the labor God has bestowed on me. God says, "You can forget the hedge at that point. I will let you be trodden down."

There are churches full of people whose lives have been trodden down by the devil because God took the hedge away when they refused to bear the fruit of righteousness. When they decided they would do what they pleased to do when they pleased, how they pleased, and they brought forth wild grapes, grapes of rebellion and pride, God said, "Okay, that is the end of the protection."

The second reason God will remove the hedge of separation is to close the mouth of Satan. The devil made accusations against Job. Most of us are not in too much danger. For most of us, if the hedge comes down, it will be because of wild grapes, not to shut the mouth of Satan, because we are not the same kind of Christian Job was. Many of us do not even want to be. God removes the hedge for testing on our part and to close the mouth of Satan.

The devil said, "Don't You know that the only reason Job serves You is because of the material blessings?" So God said, "Okay, I will remove the hedge and show you what kind of Christian he is. You do not understand. Job does not glorify Me and serve Me because of what he gets out of it. He does not serve Me because of what I do, he serves Me for who I am." God did not remove the hedge as judgment against Job, nor was it done as chastening, nor because Job had brought forth wild grapes, but He did it to get glory to Himself, and He did it to prove that the man would remain godly no matter what happened to him.

In many cases, the hedge of supplication has never even been put up. I can bear wild grapes and remove the hedge of separation. But sheer neglect will prevent there being a hedge of supplication. God said, "I sought for a man who would make up the hedge, and stand in the gap before me for the land, but I found none." God said He had to execute judgment because nobody was concerned enough to supplicate. Nobody was concerned enough to get on their face and pay the price.

In Proverbs 24:30-34 the Bible speaks of an incident similar to that. It says, *"I went by the field of the slothful, and by the vineyard of the man void of understanding; And, lo, it was all grown over with thorns, and nettles had covered the face thereof, and the stone wall thereof was broken down. Then I saw, and considered it well: I looked upon it, and received instruction. Yet a little sleep, a little*

*slumber, a little folding of the hands to sleep: So
shall thy poverty come as one that travelleth; and
thy want as an armed man."*

Homes fall apart for lack of supplication. Children
go bad for lack of supplication. Countries crumble for
lack of supplication. Sinners go to hell for lack of
supplication. Backsliders remain in their sin for lack of
supplication. I do not have to bear wild grapes. I can be
as clean as a hound's tooth and as separated as Job was,
but if I do not supplicate everything around me is going to
crumble and fall apart because there is nobody making a
hedge about it, nobody standing in the gap by way of
supplication. That is how parents can live clean and
watch their kids go to hell. They never learn the art of
supplication. They never learn the art of prevailing
prayer. They never learn the art of praying a hedge about
their loved ones.

Job was not only protected by a personal hedge,
Job went out and sacrificed for his children and supplicated for his children. He said, "Lest one of them in their
heart might have cursed God, I am going to supplicate. I
do not know that they did anything wrong, but I am going
to pray and supplicate just in case they did." His family
was protected by his supplication and his prayer. He
prayed a hedge about them.

The hedge of supplication is absent for simple neglect. If you do not have the hedge of separation you
cannot exercise the hedge of supplication. A lot of us pray
and pray for people, but the truth is, we will not separate
like Job and be clean like Job and be a servant like Job
and be peculiar like Job and be upright like Job. Have
you ever seen people that pray and pray and pray, and
their family still goes to pot? Their children still go to
hell, and everything they pray for falls apart and they
never get any answers? Do you know why? If you do not

have the hedge of separation you cannot supply the hedge of supplication for anybody else.

You must separate yourself and put yourself on praying ground inside the hedge of God's holiness where you can get answers and stand in the gap and make up the hedge for somebody else. If I will not get into God's hedge I cannot pray another hedge.

You say, "Well, Preacher, what does happen when God removes the hedge?" When God removed the hedge of separation Job lost all of his worldly possessions. That stands to reason. In II Corinthians 4:4 the Bible says the devil is the god of this world and worldly things. What he can touch has to do with material things.

The blessings of the devil are material things. I am not saying that God never gives people material things. He does. But the devil is capable of giving material things since he is the god of this world. The devil took Job's herds and his flocks and his servants. He took his home. He took his children. They were all killed in a tornado. He took Job's health. He took his position in the gate. He took his prestige in society. He put him out there on an ash heap, scraping his sores. But the thing that really floored the devil was, when Job was out there on that ash heap, scraping the oozing sores with a piece of broken pottery, he said, "Naked came I into the world, and naked shall I leave. Blessed be the name of the Lord." He bowed himself and worshiped God in spite of the fact that he had lost it all.

If Job had not been inside the hedge of protection and he had lost everything as a result of sin, he would have cursed God, just like the devil said. If he had not been the right kind of Christian he would have become bitter. He would have said, "I do not understand why God let this happen to me."

I find another hedge removed in the life of the

prodigal son. He was living at home under the protection and provision of his father. He got tired of that. He said, "Give me what falleth to me. I want my inheritance. I am going out to make it big in the world." I do not think he ever intended to end up in a hog pen. But when he left the protection and provision of his father, when he got outside of the will of the father, when he got outside of the way of holiness, he got out into a far country and the devil enticed him to live riotously. He wrecked himself and the Bible says, "he had spent all." He lost everything, his whole inheritance. Then he came to himself. When he found himself on the bottom of the barrel and was totally empty, he came to himself. What a sad time to wake up. What a sad time to realize you have erred.

That is exactly what happens when you leave the way of holiness, when you get outside the hedge of God's protection. It is just a matter of time till you lose it all. I have reasoned and pleaded with people who claimed to be saved to get into church, but they said they did not have to go to church. They could read their Bibles at home. I told one man the last time I talked to him, "Bill, you are going to lose everything." Six months later he knocked on my door to tell me a sad story. To make a long story short he said, "About a month ago I lost my job. Two weeks ago the finance company told us to move out of our house. We were three months behind when I lost my job. That is not all. My wife and I had a fuss just last night. She left and took the kids. I do not know where she is. She says she is not coming back. That is not all. I parked my car down here by the creek. Somehow it coasted down over the creek bank and smashed the whole front end on it. That is not all. I just came from the doctor's office. He told me I have bleeding ulcers."

He got outside of the hedge of God's protection. He was obstinate. I would show him what the Book said.

"God expects you to be in church. You are not to forsake the assembling of yourselves together." He said, "I do not need to go to church. I can read my Bible at home. Everything is alright. Let me alone."

God finally let him alone. And when God let him alone, the devil stripped him of everything. He lost it all.

How about Naomi? There she was, in Bethlehem-Judah, the house of bread. She got discontented. There was a famine in the land. Everything was not going smoothly. So she left Bethlehem-Judah, the house of bread. Do you know where she went? Moab, a picture of the world. God talked about Moab and called it His wash pot, or His garbage can. Do you know what she was looking for? Bread. That is rather ironic. She left the house of bread and went to the garbage can looking for bread.

While she was there she lost her two sons. First she lost her husband, Elimelech. Then she lost Malon and Chilion, her two sons. When she came back they said, "Is that Naomi?" She had aged and she was not as pretty as she once was. Sin had taken its toll. She said, *"Call me not Naomi,"* which means 'pleasant one,' *"call me Mara,"* which means 'bitter.' *"For the Almighty hath dealt very bitterly with me."* She said, *"I went out full, and the Lord hath brought me home again empty."* She said, "I left the hedge of God's protection. I left the will of God full. And the Lord hath brought me back empty."

When God takes the hedge of separation away you are going to lose it all, friend. It is just a matter of time. But let me go a step farther than that. When the hedge of supplication is not there, not only do individual lives fall apart, but nations fall apart, cities fall apart, churches fall apart, and families fall apart. You say, "Where did you get that?" I got it out of the Book of

Genesis.

I want to remind you that Sodom and Gomorrah were wicked places. Lot decided to go there to live. That was a bad choice. When God came down He came into the plains of Mamre and there was Abraham. Abraham was not in Sodom with all the pagan, heathen people, vexing his righteous soul. He was out in the plains of Mamre, separated. When God came Abraham bowed himself before Him and said, "Oh, Lord, let me kill the fatted calf. Let me minister to You. I want to commune with You, God." Abraham communed with God. He said, "Lord, what are You here for?" He said, "I am going to check Sodom out. I am going to judge the sin. The cry of Sodom is great. It is come all the way up to heaven."

Abraham knew Lot was there. He said, "Lord, if there are fifty righteous will You spare Sodom for the sake of fifty people that are saved and separated?" The Lord said, "I will spare it for fifty." Abraham said, "How about forty-five?" He said, "For forty-five I will spare it." "How about forty?" "I will spare it for forty." "How about thirty?" "I will spare it for thirty." "How about twenty?" "I will spare it for twenty." "How about ten?" "I will spare it for ten."

Lot had about eight in his family. Abraham thought surely he had two converts. Surely he had two people that had gotten saved and separated. Surely Lot had done something for God in Sodom. Surely he had led somebody to righteousness. Abraham, after supplicating and praying a hedge that would provide protection if there were just ten righteous, stopped too soon. If he would have asked for five, God would have done it for five. If he would have supplicated to the point of one, God would have done it for the sake of Lot. But Abraham stopped short. He assumed that he had prayed enough about it. He assumed that he had supplicated enough with God. He assumed that he had gone far enough.

He stopped at ten. Do you know what happened to Sodom? God burned that place off the map. I have been to Israel. I have been down to the edge of the Dead Sea where Sodom and Gomorrah, Admah and Zeboim were. I have seen the charred rock where God sent down fire from heaven and burned the place off the map. Judgment fell. Do you know why? Because there was no hedge of supplication to protect Sodom and Gomorrah. If there is not a remnant of God's people to separate and get on their faces and begin supplicating for their nation, for their city, for their family, and for their church, the wrath of God and the judgment of God is going to fall.

There is the hedge of separation. That affects individuals. If I will separate it will protect me. Then there is the hedge of supplication. That affects nations, cities, families, and churches, not just individuals. But the tragedy is if I do not separate I cannot supplicate. We have people in our churches who are trying to pray, but they are not on praying ground. They have no separation.

In II Chronicles 7:14 God said, *"If my people, which are called by my name, shall humble themselves, and pray, and seek my face, and turn from their wicked ways..."* God said in order for me to supplicate and get my prayers answered I have to separate and have the hedge of separation so that I am on praying ground for supplication.

Without the hedge of separation you cannot provide the hedge of supplication. Your family is helpless and hopeless. Your prayers are vain if you will not separate like Job, if you will not be a peculiar Christian like Job, a servant of God. He eschewed evil. He served the Lord. If you will not separate like that you can pray all you want, but without answers.

On the other hand, there are those of us who may be separated, but we are separated for nought. We have the hedge of separation. But we have missed the whole point. The reason I am supposed to separate is not just so I can say, "Boy, I am some Christian." No. I am supposed to separate so that I can put myself on praying ground so that I can supplicate. There are people who are separated and clean living, they have respect for God, but they are not prayer warriors. You are not praying a hedge about your nation, your city, your church, your pastor, or your family.

So there are two extremes. There is a crowd that prays all the time but refuses to separate. You cannot get your prayers answered. If you will not separate, you cannot supplicate effectively. On the other hand, there is a crowd that is separated but too busy to supplicate. Even though you are on praying ground you do not pray a hedge. You do not stand in the gap. God cannot find you willing. Do not kid yourself. When He said, "I sought for a man and found none," He found people who were clean living. He found people who loved Him, but He could not find anybody who was willing to supplicate, to make up the hedge and stand in the gap and be the difference for others.

Some of us need to separate. Still others of us that are separated need to begin to supplicate. There are holy hedges in the Scriptures. I thank God that if I get in the way of holiness, God says there is a hedge and the lion and the fool and the others cannot get in there. I am protected from all of that.

The only thing better than going to heaven is taking someone along. The only thing better in this life than having a hedge about myself is praying one around somebody else that I love, or the nation I love, or the church that I love, or the family and friends that I love.

Holy Hedges are available. Our families need them. Our churches need them. Our nation needs those hedges more than we ever begin to realize. Our loved ones need those hedges. But you have to separate so you can supplicate. After you are separated you have to make it a point to supplicate. You need to have these holy hedges.

CHAPTER ELEVEN

INTERCESSORY PRAYER

"Brethren, my heart's desire and prayer to God for Israel is, that they might be saved." (Romans 10:1)

As we look at Romans 10:1, we find the apostle Paul talking about his life of intercessory prayer. It is easy for you and me to pray when we have a need. It is easy for us to come to God and say, "Dear God, I need fifty dollars," or, "Dear God, I need a new car," or "I need something. Would You please provide that need?" There is nothing wrong with that kind of prayer. God wants us to depend on Him for our every need. But the tragic thing is that we do not come to God nearly often enough pleading with God for the souls of men.

The apostle Paul was a great prayer warrior. He said, *"My heart's desire and prayer to God for Israel is, that they might be saved."* He said, "I am carrying a burden on my heart. I plead with God. I pray to God. I talk with God constantly about those that are lost, pleading with God to save them."

R.A. Torrey said, "It is a great work to talk to men about God. But it is a far greater work to talk to God about men." R.A. Torrey was a great soulwinner and God used him. He did visit. He did knock on doors. He did verbalize the Gospel and tell people how to be born again, but he spent much time in his prayer closet before he went out soulwinning.

I believe that when we do not pray much for people we are very ineffective in our soulwinning labors and efforts. We have to learn this matter of intercessory prayer.

David Brainerd died at the age of twenty-nine. He

literally prayed himself to death. You say, "That was not very smart." It was not too bad. He saw thousands upon thousands of people saved because of those prayers. He accomplished more in twenty-nine years of praying and laboring in prayer than most of us accomplish in seventy years of life by knocking doors and visiting. I am not de-emphasizing the door knocking. Brainerd did go out and mix with the people. He did tell them how to be saved. He did carry the Gospel. He did preach. But he had an ingredient that you and I in many cases miss - the matter of intercessory prayer, literally coming to God with a broken heart, falling on our faces, and pouring our hearts out to God, begging and pleading with God to do what we cannot do in the hearts and lives of individuals.

When you read David Brainerd's life story or the journal that he kept, you read statements such as these: "Wednesday, April 21, God again enabled me to wrestle for numbers of souls, and had much fervency in the sweet duty of intercession." He said, "I labored today in prayer."

Most of us do not know much about laboring in prayer. Brainerd prayed until he would sweat. He prayed with tears. He prayed with fervency. In James 5:16 the Bible tells us, *"The effectual fervent prayer of a righteous man availeth much."* What kind of prayer? The effectual prayer and fervent prayer of a righteous man.

There are three things we need to look at there. Notice it needs to be the kind of prayer that has some fervency. It came from the heart. It was fervent. There was some labor, some zeal in the prayer. But it was of a righteous man. That is not just talking about a saved man. God is talking about someone who is not only born again and has God's righteousness, but has some personal righteousness.

David said it well in Psalm 66:18. He said, *"If I*

regard iniquity in my heart, the Lord will not hear me." He said, "I will not get my prayers answered. I will not be a good prayer warrior. I will not be a good intercessor if I am not willing to purge out the sin, the dross, any little thing that may be in my heart. I have to be willing to part with it. I have to be willing to confess it, forsake it, and plead the blood of Christ. I have to be willing to break with that sin before I can wrestle for souls."

That is what Brainerd knew so well. He lived a holy life. God wants you and me to live holy. Holiness is not something for years gone by. God is still holy today. He is every bit as holy as He ever has been. He still says, *"Be ye holy, for I am holy."* If you and I would purge the sin out and then come to God pleading for souls, God would do the work we cannot do. He will not go soul-winning for us, but He will certainly prepare hearts through our prayers. It makes a big difference when you have prayed much before you go out to talk to people.

Brainerd said, "On April 25, I spent about two hours in secret duties (speaking of prayer), and was enabled more than ordinarily to agonize for immortal souls. Though it was early in the morning and the sun scarcely shined at all, my body was quite wet with sweat." It was in the cool of the morning, the sun had not even risen yet, and he had already labored for two hours in prayer, so much so that he had broken a sweat in his prayer.

God wants us to learn to pray like this man prayed. He is a fine example for us. He said, "On March 14, in the morning, was almost continually engaged in prayer." "Thursday, August 4, was enabled to pray much through the whole day." "Thursday, November 3, spent this day in secret fasting and prayer from morning till night."

We read many times about great men of God like

Charles G. Finney and like David Brainerd, who did a great work with the American Indians. We read about Adoniram Judson and others, but the thing we seem to miss is the fact that they labored in prayer in order for God to give the harvest that He gave.

I believe in methods. I believe in promotion. I believe in doing anything and everything you can to get people under the sound of the Gospel, as long as it is honest. But the truth is, you and I have come to the point where we have learned to depend almost totally on methods and not at all on prayer and the power of God. We had better get back to praying and laboring in prayer, begging God and pleading with God with tears and weeping, trusting the Lord to do what man cannot do.

"Lord's Day, December 29, After public worship was over, I went to my house, proposing to preach again after a short season of intermission, but they soon came in, one after another, with tears in their eyes to know what they should do to be saved. It was an amazing season of power among them. It seemed as if God had bowed the heavens and come down and was about to convert the whole world." He said he went home after preaching. He was going to take a little time of rest and preach again, but because of the prayer life that he had, they came to his home. They came with tears streaming down their faces. They said to him, "What must I do to be saved?"

When was the last time someone came to you in tears and said, "Hey, how can I get saved?" Can you remember anybody doing that? Maybe it is because you and I have not prayed like he prayed. Maybe we do not experience that kind of power and blessing because we have not paid the same price in prayer.

There are some things that you and I are going to have to pray for if we are going to see them happen. John

Hyde, one of the greatest prayer warriors that ever lived, was known as "Praying Hyde" because he spent so much time in intercessory prayer. He wrote down in his diary, "I have felt led to pray for others this year as never before. I never knew what it was to work all day and then pray all night before God for another. Early in the morning, four or five o'clock, or even earlier, and late at night, till twelve or one o'clock, at college or at parties at home, I used to keep such hours for myself and pleasure. Can I not do as much for God and for souls?"

He said, "When I was at home I would get up early for pleasure. If it was hunting season or fishing season I would get up early. If it was a night when everybody was going to get together I would stay up till one or two o'clock for the party. Can I not do as much for God and for souls as I did for personal pleasure?"

He claimed Isaiah 62:6 as his life's verse. *"I have set watchmen upon thy walls, O Jerusalem, which shall never hold their peace day nor night: ye that make mention of the LORD, keep not silence, And give him no rest, till he establish, and till he make Jerusalem a praise in the earth."* John Hyde was continually praying for the souls of men.

He began to pray, "Dear God, I want You to give me one soul a day, saved and baptized." He prayed and begged God, and God was giving him for a great period of time one soul a day. Then he prayed, "Dear God, I will not be satisfied with one soul a day. Give me two souls a day." He prayed all the time. Every day he labored in prayer. God gave him two souls every day. Then he began to pray, "Dear God, give me three souls a day." He labored and prayed and begged. God gave him three souls a day.

He also went soulwinning, by the way. Prayer without soulwinning is incomplete. But we are incomplete in the other direction. Though most of us do not get real excited about soulwinning, when it comes time we will go, but we will not pray before we go like we ought to. Just like prayer without soulwinning is incomplete, soulwinning without prayer is incomplete. That is one of the greatest problems we have today in the church of Jesus Christ. We have forgotten how to pray. It is a lost art.

As we look back through years gone by we always say, "All those great revivals with Finney and Moody and Torrey..." Yes, and there were some great prayer warriors in those days too. And every time there has ever been a great revival anywhere in the world it has been the natural result of prayer.

There have been great revivals without much preaching. I am not lessening the importance of preaching, but there has never been a great revival where there was not much praying.

John Hyde, through his prayers, was the source of one hundred thousand people being saved in Punjab, India. Through his prayers and his labors, in that one country over one hundred thousand people came to Jesus Christ. He knew what it was to pray.

One time he prayed for Wilbur Chapman, a great evangelist. Wilbur Chapman said when he heard John Hyde pray, he realized he had never known what prayer was before.

Chapman was preaching in a little building in London, where just a few people were gathered together on the first night. The next day John Hyde came into town. He came and prayed with Wilbur Chapman. That night fifty people responded to the invitation and got saved. Why? Because of prayer along with the soulwinning, pouring our hearts out to God.

I am not just talking about going through the

motions. That is not prayer. Most of what we do is not really prayer. Most of the time when we utter words to God, we are really not fervent about it. We are really not effectual about it. We are really not burdened about it. We are really not yielding ourselves to God and pouring ourselves out to Him.

There was an American preacher who went to London to pastor. He pastored there for several years. On the first day he preached there he noticed that God had really placed his power upon him, that he had been anointed and given great power in that pulpit, more so than ever before when he preached.

Several years later he was called to the bedside of an old man with a weak voice. That old man said, "Pastor, I do not tell you this for any other reason but that hopefully someone will pick up where I left off. The first night that you came to our town God moved on my heart and I spent that Saturday night, all night, without sleep in prayer, praying for the power of God on your ministry. Every single Saturday night since you came here, I have stayed up all night Saturday night and pleaded and begged with God in prayer for God's power to be upon you and for God to use you."

That old man, with a weak voice, breathed out his last few breaths. He said, "I hope that someone will take up the work of intercession." That preacher realized that the great power he had had in that pulpit was not because of his dynamic personality, nor was it because of his greatness, but because there was somebody pouring out his heart to God faithfully for God's power to be upon his life and ministry.

I do not think we realize just how important it is for us to be a praying people. God says power comes through prayer.

We talk about Charles G. Finney. I do not suppose

there was ever a greater evangelist or revivalist than Charles G. Finney. He was used of God because he believed in the spirit of prayer. He talked about the spirit of prayer and about people being in the spirit of prayer.

He also had a little old man who travelled with him called Father Nash. That old man would spend literally hours upon hours upon hours pleading with God and weeping. Finney held a meeting in Rochester, New York. During that meeting there were one hundred thousand people saved and added to the churches. The meeting lasted more than a year and Father Nash spent hours every single day pouring his heart out to God, pleading with God for souls.

There was another man that Finney talked about. His name was Abel Clarey. Nobody knew him. He was a preacher, but he seldom preached. He was a prayer warrior. Sometimes he would be so weakened from prayer, he would pray so strenuously and for so long and give himself so heavily to prayer, that he would not even come out in public. Now if he were around today we would think he was backslidden because he did not make it to one of the services. That man was the source of power in many cases for Charles G. Finney's meetings because he literally poured himself out and gave himself in intercession for souls. He knew what it was to weep. He knew what it was to cry. He knew what it was to plead. He knew what it was to pray with fervency and zeal. For hours upon hours he would pour his heart out to God.

The Great Awakening in America, in the New England states, was the result of Jonathan Edward's famous call to prayer. He often said, "We have to get back to prayer. We have to get back to praying. We have to get back to pleading with God for the souls of men." It got a hold of some ministers' hearts. It got a hold of some people's hearts. As a result of his call to prayer, the Great Awakening took place and a great revival broke out in the New England states. Thousands of people were saved because the people of God once again learned to pray.

We talk about Charles Spurgeon and the great ministry he had. But as we look back through the pages of history, as we look at biographies, we find that Charles Spurgeon many times had fifty or sixty men in the basement praying every time he stepped into the pulpit. The whole time he preached, while he stood in the pulpit, there were fifty men on their faces pleading with God, begging God for power, begging God for souls. That is where power comes from.

D.L. Moody spoke in London. He knew that greater power was upon his life and his ministry than normal. He asked the pastor, "Do you have any members who are not here? Do you have any members who are not able to come to the meeting?" The pastor said, "Yes, but why?" He said, "Somebody, somewhere is praying. I want to find that person." D.L. Moody began to visit the shut ins.

He found a little old lady. She could not come to the services. She was crippled and was in bad health. She said, "Mr. Moody, I have been begging God for three years to send you here. I have been pleading with God day and night for revival to break out and for souls to be saved. How is the meeting going?" He told her of the great numbers saved, five hundred saved in one service. Tears burst out of her eyes and rolled down her cheeks. Moody began to weep as well. She said, "Mr. Moody, God is honoring those years of prayer." And he always does, if we will put those years of prayer to work. That little old lady who was praying made the difference.

We talk about Dr. Jack Hyles and others who are alive and on the scene today and have the power of God in that way. We talk about the great ministries that they have. Did you know that every time Brother Hyles steps into the pulpit there is a little old lady who has his schedule and knows where he is, knows what the time zone is, knows when he is stepping up to preach, and when he sits down from preaching? All the time he is in the pulpit, that little woman spends every moment on her knees, pleading with God and begging for God's power.

Intercession is a lost art. There is nothing that your church cannot have that the church in Acts chapter two had. Everything they had, the power, the blessing, the souls, you can have it and I can have it. But what happened in Acts chapter two is a result of Acts 1:14. The Bible says that they were all gathered together, and for days they prayed and they poured their hearts out to God. They pleaded and they begged God. Then in Acts 2:41 the Bible says they reaped as a result of their prayer. They went soulwinning too. But they went soulwinning after they had saturated their minds and their hearts and the area with prayer.

Souls get saved because of prayer. I believe everybody who gets saved gets saved because someone is praying somewhere. Backsliders get restored because of intercessory prayer. Revivals break out because of intercessory prayer. Churches are built and raised up by God because of intercessory prayer. Great preachers are raised up because of intercessory prayer among the people of God.

God still raises sick people up, not by thumping them in the head, but by intercessory prayer. You don't need to have a healing line. Just get on your knees and begin to plead and beg and pray and trust God. He is still a miracle working God. I am not going to let the charismatics steal the fact that God is powerful from me. I am not involved in any of that wild fire, but there is a

God in heaven who is able to do anything He ever did. The problem is He is looking for someone to intercede. He is looking for someone to stand in the gap.

It is not just standing in the gap talking to people about God, but standing in the gap talking to God about people. God is looking for someone to make up the hedge. He is looking for someone to be the deterrent to sin and evil.

You and I can elect the right guy every time, but that is not going to change America. It is going to take a praying people. We need to intercede for this nation of ours. We need to intercede for our leaders. We need to intercede for souls.

It amazes me, I find all over this country folks who complain about their preacher but never pray for him. If you would pray for the man of God as much as you gripe about him, you would not have anything to gripe about.

The Bible says that what God wants us to learn to do is to intercede and pour our hearts and our souls out so that God can honor and bless it.

I am talking about Romans 10:1 praying. I am talking about James 5:16 praying. I am talking about Matthew 7:7 praying; asking, seeking, and knocking, laboring in prayer. I am talking about II Chronicles 7:14 praying. *"If my people, which are called by my name, shall humble themselves, and pray, and seek my face, and turn from their wicked ways; then will I hear from heaven, and will forgive their sin, and will heal their land."*

I am talking about watching and praying. I mean doing without sleep sometimes and praying. I mean staying up a little bit later in prayer, maybe all night sometimes. I am talking about getting up a little bit earlier and praying. I am talking about fasting and praying. God wants us to learn to fast and pray.

Are souls really important? Is there really a need? Is there a hell? Are people going to hell? If so, if the Bible be true, and if there be a God in heaven, and if there is a hell, how could sleep and food be more important than prayer for souls? I am not talking about starving yourself to death. I am not talking about going without sleep for months and destroying yourself. I am talking about paying a price sometimes, proving your sincerity, doing what is necessary. I am talking about weeping in prayer. When was the last time you got on your knees and prayed for someone else? I do not mean when everything seemed like the world was caving in on you and you got on your knees and wept. I do not mean when you were praying for your own needs and your heart was heavy. I mean, when was the last time you actually got on your face before God and wept over souls? wept over your family? wept over your loved ones?

My uncle was a drunkard, a hard case. I witnessed to him dozens of times. I prayed for him often, but I have never been as faithful to pray for my uncle as my dad was. My dad, since the day he got saved, prayed for my uncle every single day. My dad witnessed to him almost weekly. He talked to him all the time about the Lord, and lived it before him. He prayed and pleaded with God fervently for him and all of his brothers.

A few years ago, my uncle got sick and was in the hospital. My dad went over to talk to him and was witnessing to him about the Lord. He said, "Donny, you know you are not saved. You ought to settle that." Donny said, "Yeah, I have been waiting for you to come over. I am going to settle that tonight." He got on his knees and prayed, trusted Christ and got saved.

He had been going to church as much as possible. His health was not good. Everybody in town said they could not believe it. He was a changed man. Five weeks later he was getting ready for Wednesday night prayer meeting. He bent down to buckle his shoes and collapsed on the floor.

They took him to the hospital and in about four or five days he was gone out into eternity. I thought and I wondered, "What if my dad had been no more faithful to pray for him than I was?"

It is easy for you and me to pray for our needs. But God wants us to have enough character to pray for others' needs and to be as burdened and broken as if it were us we were praying for.

I gave my uncle every argument there was from the Scriptures why he ought to get saved, but he would not do it. The prayers of my dad made the difference. I believe that with all of my heart.

Jesus set the example in prayer. The Bible says that many times He spent all night in prayer. Some of the last words we hear from the Son of God were those words on Calvary, as He hung there about to die, interceding for His enemies. *"Father, forgive them, for they know not what they do."* He was concerned about those that hated Him the most.

When we look at John chapter 17 we find the Lord Jesus praying. He said, "I pray, not that you would take them out of the world, but that you would keep them in the world." What was He doing? He was praying for His disciples.

Something dawned on me one day. We are always trying to find new methods for conserving converts. There are some things we can do that are practical. But Paul said something in Galatians 4:19. He said, *"I travail in birth again until Christ be formed in you."* Paul had the same fervor, the same zeal, the same burden, the same brokenness in prayer over his converts after they got saved as he did to get them saved. He wept over them. He travailed again. He travailed once to get them saved. But Paul said, "I did not quit travailing when you got saved. I travail again that Christ might be formed in you."

Jesus Christ set the example. He interceded for His disciples. He interceded for His enemies. He interceded for the lost. He pleaded with His Father in heaven to meet the need.

As I look at Genesis chapter 18, I find a beautiful story about a man named Abraham. In verses 23-33 we find that Abraham begged and pleaded with God for Sodom. He said, "Dear God, if You find ten righteous, will you spare it for the ten's sake?" He started with fifty, and then forty, and thirty and twenty, and finally ten. If he had taken it down to three, I believe God would have honored his prayer and Sodom would have remained. He quit too soon. I am not criticizing him, but had he gone as far as three, God would have gone with him. But where he stopped, God stopped. He pleaded and he begged.

God agreed. He said, "If I find ten righteous, just as many as ten righteous people in all of Sodom and Gomorrah, I will spare the whole land for the sake of the ten." Intercession.

George Mueller, one of the greatest prayer warriors that ever lived, prayed for three men. He prayed for the first of those men for sixty years and the man was saved. He prayed for another for sixty-two years and Mueller died. At Mueller's funeral that man was saved. There was another man that Mueller prayed for for those sixty-two years, and that third man was saved two years after Mueller's burial.

You say, "Well, he was already gone. It was not his prayer." Do not tell me that stuff. The Bible says, "And their works do follow them." He had a ministry in prayer.

That man prayed down seven million dollars in his lifetime, and not a penny of it for selfish purposes. Every bit of it went to little orphan children and presenting the Gospel of Jesus Christ.

Mueller did not quit too soon. Abraham dropped off at ten and Sodom was destroyed. But Mueller prayed until the day of his death, interceding for those men. All three of them were saved as a result of his prayers.

When you look at the Word of God you see that Paul was probably one of the greatest prayer warriors. In Romans 9:1-3, Paul said, *"I say the truth in Christ, I lie not, my conscience also bearing me witness in the Holy Ghost, That I have great heaviness and continual sorrow in my heart. For I could wish that myself were accursed from Christ for my brethren, my kinsmen according to the flesh."* Paul said, "I carry a continual burden in my heart. I am always burdened. My heart is always heavy."

He did not say he did not enjoy life. He did not say he was not happy. He did not say he did not have the joy of the Lord, but he said, "There is something that weighs heavily on my heart. There is something awesome and serious about those that are going to hell. I would be willing, if it were possible, to die and go to hell for them that they might be saved." That was his heartbeat. That was his burden. That was the kind of fervency he prayed with.

When Paul came to God he pleaded with Him. He was so involved and so concerned he would have been willing to go to hell for those he was praying for if it would have been possible to take their place.

The Bible talks over and over about Paul's prayer life. Something stands out about the life of Paul in every single epistle that he writes. In Romans 1:8-9 he says, *"First, I thank my God through Jesus Christ for you all, that your faith is spoken of throughout the whole world. For God is my witness, whom I serve with my spirit in the gospel of his Son, that without ceasing I make mention of you always in my prayers."* He told the people at Rome,"I pray for you all the time. Every day when I pray, I pray for you."

In I Corinthians 1:4 Paul said, *"I thank my God always on your behalf, for the grace of God which is given you by Jesus Christ."* He said, "I thank God for you. Every time I pray I am always praying for you."

In II Corinthians 13:7 he made a similar statement. He said, *"Now I pray to God that ye do no evil; not that we should appear approved, but that ye should do that which is honest, though we be as reprobates."* Paul said, "I am praying for you. I am begging God that you will tow the line. I am interceding for you that God will help you to live the Christian life."

When you look at the Book of Ephesians, in chapter one, verses 15-17, you find the same thing again. *"Wherefore I also, after I heard of your faith in the Lord Jesus, and love unto all the saints, Cease not to give thanks for you, making mention of you in my prayers."*

In Philippians 1:2-4 Paul said, *"Grace be unto you, and peace, from God our Father, and from the Lord Jesus Christ. I thank my God upon every remembrance of you, Always in every prayer of mine for you all making request with joy."* He said, "I am praying for you. I am pleading with God. I am interceding for you."

In Colossians 1:3 he said, *"We give thanks to God and the Father of our Lord Jesus Christ, praying always for you."* I Thessalonians 1:2 says, *"We give thanks to God always for you all, making mention of you in our prayers."* II Thessalonians 1:3 says, *"We are bound to thank God always for you, brethren, as it is meet, because that your faith groweth exceedingly, and the charity of every one of you all toward each other aboundeth."* I Timothy 2:1 says, *"I exhort therefore, that, first of all, supplications, prayers, intercessions, and giving of thanks, be made for all men."*

Paul prayed, and he encouraged those he wrote to to do the same thing. Notice II Timothy 1:3. Paul said, *"I thank God, whom I serve from my forefathers with pure conscience, that without ceasing I have remembrance of thee in my prayers night and day."*

In the Book of Philemon, in verse four Paul said, *"I thank my God, making mention of thee always in my prayers."*

Paul was concerned enough to pray, and he did it with tears. He did it with weeping. He did it with a broken heart. He did it with sincerity and with zeal, and with all that was in him.

In Acts 7:54-60, we find Stephen. I believe Stephen's prayer of intercession made the difference in the apostle Paul's conversion. I believe it was because of Stephen's spirit of prayer and because of his love for God and the sweet spirit about him in his death, because he prayed, *"Lord, lay not this sin to their charge."*

In verse 54 it says, *"When they heard these things they were cut to the heart."* That is conviction. They gnashed upon him with their teeth. *"But he, being full of the Holy Ghost, looked up stedfastly into heaven, and saw the glory of God, and Jesus standing on the right hand of God, And said, Behold, I see the heavens opened, and the Son of man standing on the right hand of God. Then they cried out with a loud voice, and stopped their ears, and ran upon him with one accord, And cast him*

out of the city, and stoned him: and the witnesses
laid down their clothes at a young man's feet, whose
name was Saul. And they stoned Stephen, calling
upon God, and saying, Lord Jesus, receive my spirit.
And he kneeled down, and cried with a loud voice,
Lord, lay not this sin to their charge." What was he
doing? He was interceding for his enemies. He was
pleading for their very souls.

God gave them to him, too. The great apostle Paul,
I believe, was a direct result of that prayer right there.
That man who knew God so well and walked with God so
much could even intercede for his enemies, pleading for
God to forgive them for their sin.

I am a direct result of my parents' prayers. If it
were not for my parents' prayers, I might be in hell
tonight. I did not want to hear anything they had to say.
But I would come in at night and hear them in the
bedroom, pleading with God, begging God to save me.
Whether I had heard it or not it would have had its effect.

Week in and week out they prayed and they
pleaded with God. God honored their prayers. That is
why I stand here tonight, because of faithful parents who
prayed for me.

Some of you parents have wayward children. You
say, "What do you do? They will not listen." Pray them
in. Intercede. Do not give up. Pour your heart out to
God. Fast and pray, weep and pray, watch and pray.
Pray with some fervency.

I was invited to preach at the Beth Haven high
school chapel when I was in Bible college. I jumped at
the opportunity. I went into the office and said, "Could I
have a list of every student's name in this school?" They
said, "Yes. But why?" There were seven hundred
students. I said, "I would like to have a list so I could
pray for them."

I carried that list home and every morning I got up good and early. I prayed by name for those seven hundred students. Every night before I went to bed I prayed over the names of those seven hundred students. I begged God for power.

I got up in that chapel service. When I finished preaching I could have wept because the sermon was so bad. I thought, "Good night. All that fasting. Eight days. All that praying. All in vain. Nobody will get saved from a message like that. Nobody will respond to that."

I gave an invitation and four or five or six of those students came down the aisle and got saved. During the day, several others came to their teachers and got saved. The altar was filled with young people who had not moved all year long.

They had big name preachers in there all year long. Those kids would not move. I got up and preached the worst sermon they had heard all year long. It was the sorriest sermon they had heard all year long, but they walked the aisle. Why? Intercession. Prayer. Pleading and praying by name specifically. Fasting and praying.

Three of us covenanted together to pray and fast in Ohio. There was a fella who was a drunk and his brother. They would never come to church. On Monday night I came into town and we covenanted to fast and pray. On Wednesday night, to make a long story short, we had said we would not break the fast until those fellas got saved. We started on Tuesday, and on Wednesday, after only two days of fasting, one of those brothers came down the aisle weeping. He looked like he was fighting a sand storm. He fell on the altar and got saved.

The next night, the other brother was there. The invitation started. He stood to his feet halfway through the invitation. He burst into tears, came out and ran down the aisle, fell on the altar and got saved.

Why? Not because it was a good sermon. Because several people had banded together and had been fasting and praying, pleading with God for the souls of those two men. Intercession.

There was a woman in Jacksonville, Florida. I preached a sermon on prayer on a Sunday morning. She had a sailor husband who was in Massachusetts. He did not want anything to do with God. I preached on fasting and praying. I preached on watching and praying. I preached on praying with tears and I preached on continually praying, without ceasing, not giving up.

That little woman believed what I preached. She went home and began to plead and pray for God to save her husband. She fasted one day, then the next night she spent all night in prayer.

The next morning her husband called. He said, "I want to know Jesus. You tell me how to know Him." He was weeping on the other end of the line. She did not call him. He called her from a thousand miles away, up in Massachusetts. Today he is a preacher of the Gospel.

I just believe there is a God in heaven that loves people and wants to answer prayer and wants folks to know that He exists. He wants you and me to know He is real, that is why He wants us to pray. He wants to do things for you. He wants to save your loved ones. He wants to send revival. He wants to meet our needs.

I believe God cannot resist when His children fall on their faces, begging and pleading with Him.

I read a little story about a man who was on watch duty during the Civil War. He had fallen asleep on watch. He was condemned to die because he was sleeping on watch.

Several people came to Abraham Lincoln, who was a very compassionate man. They said, "Mr. Lincoln, would you please let the man go free?"

Mr. Lincoln wanted to let him go free, but he thought it best that the punishment be carried out to keep others from being slothful in their duty.

Off in the corner of the room was Lincoln's little son, Tad. He heard the conversation. He came over to his dad with big tears welled up in his eyes. He said, "Please, Dad, please let him go free for my sake." The man never got executed. He went free. Why? Because Lincoln could not resist the plea of his son.

You and I can come to our Heavenly Father and beg and plead for God to save people, and He will. We need to learn the art of intercession.

CHAPTER TWELVE

PRAYING FOR THE LOST

"I exhort therefore, that, first of all, supplications, prayers, intercessions, and giving of thanks, be made for all men; For kings, and for all that are in authority; that we may lead a quiet and peaceable life in all godliness and honesty. For this is good and acceptable in the sight of God our Saviour; Who will have all men to be saved, and to come unto the knowledge of the truth." (I Timothy 1:1-4)

God wants to save people. In our text He gives a direct correlation between our prayers of intercession and people being saved. He said He wants us to pray for all men, and then just two verses later He says, "For God would have all men to be saved." God does not want anyone to die and go to hell. Prayer is a vital instrument in the hand of God to save sinners. I hope I can convince you of that. I hope I can challenge you to pray like you have never prayed for lost people.

The Bible says in James 5:16, *"The effectual fervent prayer of a righteous man availeth much."* It means, "It makes a big difference. It will help to get a job done." But it has to be *"the effectual fervent prayer of a righteous man."* That is a mouth full. When he talks about a righteous man, he is not only talking about imputed righteousness that we get at salvation, but he is also talking about personal righteousness. When he talks about fervency, he is talking about heat and intensity. He is talking about a zeal and a fervor in my prayer life. The truth is the average Christian has not spent much time in prayer at all, and when he has, there has been no heat, no fervency, no tears have been shed, no wrestling in the prayer closet.

We know little about wrestling for the souls of men in prayer. We are not going to reach our cities, we are not going to have revival, and we are not going to accomplish what we dream of doing in fundamentalism until we really learn to pray.

Samuel took prayer so seriously that he said, *"God forbid that I should sin against the Lord in ceasing to pray for you."* He said, "It is the will of God that I pray for you and intercede for you." He was talking to some folks who were not doing everything they were supposed to do. He was talking to some people who were totally outside of the will of God. To fail in prayer for others is to sin.

God said that we are supposed to pray for all men, and the reason that we are supposed to pray for all men is because God wants all men to be saved. The effectual fervent prayer of a righteous man availeth much. I believe that everyone who is born again gets saved because of somebody somewhere praying. I believe that prayer is an instrument used by God to bring conviction on the hearts and souls of men to bring them to Christ. The right kind of prayer by the right kind of person avails much.

If you taped your prayer life, you would have two shocking revelations. Number one, you would be shocked at how little tape it took. Number two, you would be shocked at how often you pray for yourself, and how seldom you pray for anybody else, especially for the lost. There are one hundred and sixty-eight hours in the week, and the average person does not spend five minutes a day before the throne of God. That is about thirty-five minutes a week, out of one hundred and sixty-eight hours.

The fact that *"prayer...availeth much"* could not be better illustrated than it is in the life of John Newton, the songwriter who penned the words to "Amazing

Grace." He once was a slave trader on a ship, a very wicked young man. All the time that he was growing up his mother prayed for him every day until she died. His father was not a Christian. When John's mother died, his father began to rear him, but it was not until after John was grown that his father got saved. From the time that John's father got saved until he died, he prayed for John's salvation every single day.

There was a young lady who knew John as a young boy. Her name was Mary. She would one day become John Newton's wife. For all those years in his absence, every single day, that young woman prayed for the soul of John Newton, that God would spare him, and that God would save him. Did their prayers avail much? Well, he continued to live wickedly for years. He was a blasphemer. He was an immoral, ungodly man. But there is something I think you ought to know about our prayers. So many times we pray for somebody and we think because they do not get saved immediately that our prayers are having no impact whatsoever. It may just be that the fact that they are still alive and still have an opportunity to be saved is the result of your prayers.

When John Newton was on board the ship there were numerous times when storms would rise up. Others his age, in the same situation, died before his eyes, yet he was always spared. Somehow John Newton was always missed by the huge waves that swept over the boat in the storm, though someone standing right beside him vanished from sight into the sea. There were others on the ship like John, who were no more sinful and wicked than he was, yet they died lost, and went to hell. Could it be that those were the poor, wretched souls who had nobody back home to pray for them? Were they so unfortunate as to have nobody to intercede for them and plead their cases before the throne of God?

John Newton did not get saved right away, and he lived a number of years in wickedness and dissipation, but he had many close brushes with death in those years. Death was before him all the time. I believe the reason that he did not die and go to hell, the reason that he lived long enough to get saved is because somebody was praying. It availed much even though they did not get an immediate answer to their prayer for his salvation. You say, "Oh, God, save so-and-so." You pray for that lost sinner, but you do not see him turning to Christ. Do not get discouraged and quit. It may be your prayers that are allowing that one to live long enough to have one more opportunity to get saved. It may be that your prayers are availing much, and are the only thing that keeps them from perishing while others around them perish.

On one occasion there was a rebellion of a shipload of slaves. There were always many more slaves than there were sailors. When the rebellion took place John had a close call. The crew was being murdered one by one, but just before they got to John, some of his men got guns and killed every single slave. There were records of such rebellions on other ships where entire crews and captains were killed and the slaves took over the ship and went back to their homeland. But God spared the life of John Newton.

On another occasion he was captured by a mob and nearly killed in town, but once again his life was spared. Those who were praying for his salvation, those who were praying for his soul did not know the circumstances he was going through, but their prayers availed much. Others were killed when John Newton was in the same situation and released.

On one occasion he was placed into slavery himself, and nearly starved to death while suffering with jungle fever. He was tortured and ridiculed and given no food while he watched his captors dine. He did not think he would make it off of that island alive, but again, he was spared. I believe somebody's prayers availed much.

It sounds to me like the effectual fervent prayers of some righteous people were availing much. Was he saved yet? No, but their prayers were availing. He lived on to have another day to get saved. He lived on to have another opportunity to hear the Gospel and repent and turn to Christ. You had better be careful when you get discouraged about those loved ones you pray for over the course of weeks and months and maybe even years. You had better not abandon them. It may be that your prayers are the only thing that stands between them and death and hell. Although you have not had the answer you are expecting, God may be using your prayers in a greater way than you ever imagined. Do not be discouraged about praying for the lost, though they do not immediately repent.

John Newton was once lost in the jungle. He and another man searched for a way out of the jungle until they were totally exhausted and hungry and sick. They sat down in desperation. It looked like there was no hope. As they sat there they saw a light and were able to find their way out of the jungle and to the shore. After days of wandering, they suddenly found a way out. The other man who accompanied John was amazed by the seemingly miraculous deliverance, and said to him, "God must want us alive for some reason."

Once he was drunk on the ship. His hat blew off and he dove after it. He could not even swim. But in a drunken stupor he jumped overboard. The other sailors assumed that he had already drowned because they did not see him or hear from him. They were too intoxicated to do or care much about it. About an hour later they heard some noise. They looked over the ship and found a drunken John Newton hanging there by his coat on a loose board that was sticking out. Was he saved yet? No, but he was salvaged. Somebody's prayers were availing much.

In order for people to get saved they have to be salvaged long enough to come to repentance. It may be that your prayers do not result in an immediate conversion, but it may be that your prayers allow them to live long enough to come to Jesus Christ, long enough to get a broken will, long enough to repent and receive the Savior. Our prayers are instrumental in both salvaging men and purchasing time for them, and in bringing them to a place of repentance.

On one occasion there was a mutiny planned on his ship led by two men. They decided they were going to kill John Newton, who was at that time the captain of the ship. Within hours of when the mutiny was to begin, one of those men became ill and died suddenly. The second man and the rest of the crew agreed that they would continue as planned and kill Newton. On the following day, a storm arose unexpectedly, and the second man who led the mutiny was swept overboard to his death by a huge wave. Say anything you like, but the effectual fervent prayer of a righteous man availeth much. He was about to be killed, a mutiny was in progress, and both of those who were the leaders of the mutiny were taken out of the way.

Finally God began to get ahold of John Newton's heart. Everything on the voyage had gone wrong, and it seemed that death was closer with every moment. They weathered a storm that seemed as if it would surely sink the ship. When the storm finally subsided, the ship had sustained so much damage that water had to be pumped out constantly, and it would barely sail. When the boat began to sink, he cried out, "God, if You will let me live I will come to Christ, I will get saved." Finally, in answer to many, many prayers, John Newton trusted the Lord Jesus Christ.

Shortly after his conversion experience they headed for Ireland in their battered ship. When they finally limped into harbor and anchored the ship, they barely got to shore before another storm arose, capsized the ship, and sank it in the harbor before their eyes. On that very trip three men had starved to death, but John Newton was spared, and finally, was saved.

John Newton's mother died praying for him, and his father died praying for him, and their prayers availed beyond the grave. The Bible says, *"Their works do follow them."* Intercession is a work that will follow you. Your intercessory prayers will outlive you. Those things that you bind in the presence of God, and those prayers that you pray will outlive you. That is one work that will follow you. It will go beyond the extension of your lifetime. There are several beautiful illustrations of that verse in Scripture and in the stories of godly people.

His mother had also prayed for many years that he would end up being a preacher. For many years that looked like a foolish prayer. His father prayed for the same thing. She had prayed that he would marry that young Christian lady named Mary Catlett. John returned to England, married Mary Catlett and surrendered to preach the Gospel of Jesus Christ. He wrote the song "Amazing Grace," that you and I sing almost as our theme song. "Amazing Grace, how sweet the sound that saved a wretch like me. I once was lost, but now am found, was blind, but now I see."

John Newton was the trophy of somebody's prayers. Do you think he was any less deserving of hell than those who were swept overboard? Do you think he deserved to be spared? He was not spared because he deserved it any more than the others. He did not live on while others died in his presence because he deserved it. He lived because somebody paid the price in the prayer closet on his behalf. I wonder what would have happened if those other men had somebody back home praying and interceding for them, somebody that loved God and knew how to make intercession. Maybe they, too, would have been spared. I believe that everyone who is spared, and everyone who is saved is a result of God answering prayer. It may not even be the prayer of someone that knows me intimately, but somebody that has a line to God, that is an effectual fervent prayer warrior, that prays for me. God honors that.

In the Old Testament we find Abraham interceding for Sodom. You know the story. Lot had cast his tent toward Sodom. Abraham was out in the plains of Mamre. He was separated from the ungodly world. He was a clean man. When the Lord came along, Abraham wanted to do sacrifice. He said to the Lord, "Where are You going?" He said, "We are going to Sodom to see the wickedness. If it is as bad as it is supposed to be, We are going to destroy it." Abraham said, "But what about those righteous people in Sodom? Will You destroy the righteous with the wicked? What if there are fifty righteous? Will You spare Sodom for the fifty?" The Lord said, "Yes, I will spare it for fifty's sake."

Then Abraham said, "What about for forty-five? What if they are shy five? Will You spare it for the forty-five's sake? or will You also destroy those forty-five righteous?" God said, "I will spare it for the sake of forty-five." Abraham said, "What if there are only forty? Will You spare it for the sake of forty?" God said, "I will spare it for the sake of forty." Abraham said, "God, what if there are thirty? Will You please spare it for the sake of thirty?" God said, "I will spare it for thirty." Abraham said, "Now Lord, do not be angry with me, but what if there are only twenty? Will You spare it for the sake of the twenty?" God said, "I will spare it for the twenty."

Abraham said, "Let me speak just once more. Do not be angry with me, God, but what if there are ten righteous?" God said, "If there are ten righteous, I will spare all the land of Sodom and Gomorrah. I will not burn them off the map if there are just ten righteous." Did you notice, Abraham did not have to twist God's arm? All that Sodom needed was somebody to intercede. If Abraham would have gone down to five, I believe that God would have gone down to five. If Abraham would have gone to one, God would have gone to one. God wants us to learn to intercede because our prayers make a difference.

Abraham's prayers, the prayers of one man who had separated himself from the ungodly world, made it so that if there were only ten righteous men Sodom would have been spared. If I read it right, Lot had eight in his family, including his in-laws. Abraham thought, "Surely he has one or two converts besides his family." Abraham stopped short. I am not faulting him, but I am telling you that if he had gone down to five, and three, and two, and one, God would have spared the cities for the sake of those few that were righteous. Though he was back-slidden and had left the will of God, Sodom could have been spared for Lot. I believe that God is looking for more than just imputed righteousness.

God honored Abraham's prayer. We are allowing America to go to hell, and we are allowing our loved ones to die and go to hell, and we are allowing sinners to perish eternally because we are a prayerless generation and we are not praying for all men. For the most part, we are not praying for anybody but ourselves.

In Exodus chapter thirty-two, the children of Israel

were living in wickedness. Moses came down and found them naked, and worshiping a golden calf. He found them in every kind of wickedness and folly that you can imagine. God said, "Step back, Moses, I am going to kill the whole bunch and start over with you." God said, "That is it. Judgment is determined. They deserve judgment." Moses fell on his face and said, "God, please, if You are going to blot them out, blot me out of Your book too. Please spare them God, for my sake. If You will not spare them, do not spare me either." And God spared them. When they deserved judgment, when judgment was determined, the intercessory prayer of Moses made the difference, it stemmed the tide.

In Ezekiel chapter twenty-three the Bible says that God is looking for a man that would make up the hedge and stand in the gap before Him for the land. I believe in soulwinning. I preach soulwinning. I practice soulwinning, but you hear me. That verse is not talking about soulwinning. That verse is talking about me making up the hedge, and standing in the gap for the land. I am interceding before the throne of God as a priest for the land.

The prophet went out into the land and represented God. That is what a prophet does. The prophet takes the Word of God and proclaims it. He is preaching the truth and tries to tell people about God. The priest stands in the gap before God for the land, for the people. He intercedes in prayer. God said, *"I sought for a man who would make up the hedge and stand in the gap before me for the land, but I found none."* After that he said, "Therefore, because of this, judgment is determined." He goes on to tell us that the land would be judged because no one was making up the hedge and standing in the gap. No one was interceding. No one was praying for the people or the land. I am afraid that

America is in that kind of trouble with God today.

When Moses got his prayer answered, he said to the people, *"Who is on the Lord's side? Let him come unto me."* God spared everybody initially. To the ones who came over Moses said, "You go on out with your swords and get rid of the rest of these rebels." Judgment still came to the rebels. Ultimately, it came to them, but there was an initial holding back to give them time to make a decision. Moses bought them some time by making intercession.

When Jesus was on Calvary He prayed for his enemies. *"Father, forgive them, for they know not what they do."* Maybe the reason He said that was because the sword of the Lord was drawn at that point to destroy those wicked men. It would not have changed the work at Calvary. God would not have stunned the progress of Calvary, but have you ever noticed how many times in the Old Testament God used some heathen nation to judge His people, and then judged the heathen nation afterwards? God may have been ready to let judgment fall upon those who crucified our Lord, and if that is so, the prayer of Jesus salvaged them. The Lord Jesus may have bought some of those folks time, like the centurion who said, "Surely, this was the Son of God." I believe that old boy got saved.

I remember hearing Joe Boyd tell about his mother praying for him. He had already been saved when he was twelve, but he never consecrated his life, he never got right with God until he was twenty-seven years old. Once he was out in the ship yard, playing cards late into the night. While he was gambling a hurricane came in that lifted the roof off of the building and stuck the wind gauge at one hundred and sixty-eight miles an hour. Brother Boyd said when that roof came off he heard a voice that said, "Son, if you do not straighten up, I am

going to kill you." It scared him and he went on home.
But after several weeks had passed he talked himself out
of it. He said, "I was just scared. It was just the wind."

He was out there gambling another time, late into
the night. He said he picked his cards up and looked at
them, but he could not see what was on the cards. All he
could see was his mother praying for him. He looked
again and that was all he could see. They said, "Joe, it is
your play." He threw down his cards and said, "I am out.
I am going home." He got into his car and started across
the causeway. But on the way across he fell asleep and
wrecked, and he heard that voice again, "Son, if you do
not straighten up, I am going to kill you."

He got out of his car and made his way to an old
preacher who had influenced him. He got himself right
with God and surrendered his life. That mother praying
for him day in and day out was the very one, I believe,
that kept him alive long enough to be what he is today.
He was living a wicked life and deserved judgment. But
her prayers availed much when he did not deserve to be
spared. He was spared because of her prayers.

I think about my mother and dad praying for me.
They were saved about six months before I was, and they
began to witness to me and pray for me. Sometimes I
would come home at one or two o'clock in the morning
and I would hear them in their bedroom on their knees,
praying for me. They were crying, "Oh, God, please save
Denny." I was a wicked old rascal who deserved to die
and go to hell.

I was a bouncer in a bar room. I remember nights
there when they would hang their coats up in the coat
room and guns would fall out of the pockets of the
clientele. One night I threw a fella out and he ended up
stabbing a guy after they got outside. The bouncer who
was there before I was nearly got killed. That is why I

took the job.

I was in several car wrecks just in that six month period before I got saved. One time the car rolled nine times and hit a tree fifteen feet in the air. It snapped the tree off and landed on its roof. We were going over one hundred miles an hour. What happened? God preserved me. I believe that God was answering prayer, and salvaged my life. In another car accident, all of us were out there living like a bunch of drunks. None of us were fit to drive. I was not going to drive. My friend said he could, but he could not. He wrecked my car dead into a tree, going about seventy miles an hour. What happened? I had to get the rear view mirror scraped out of my left arm, but I had no serious debilitating injuries. God spared me again.

For six months after Mom and Dad got saved they prayed for me. I rebelled and got meaner by the month, because their prayers were affecting me and I was miserable and under conviction. That last month I was in total rebellion. I was arrested three times. I smashed up several places. The Holy Ghost of God was still working on me. When they started witnessing I could walk away, but I could not get away from the effect of their prayers. I am thankful to God I could not run far enough or hard enough or fast enough to get away from it, for if I had outrun the effect of their prayers I probably would have died and gone to hell.

Finally I went to the little church they attended and listened to a Gospel message. That night I went into my bedroom, got on my knees, and asked the Lord to save me. I believe I stand here today, saved and serving the Lord, as a result of their prayers.

God said there needs to be intercession made for all men. Why? Because God will have all men to be saved, and your intercession availeth much. Even if they do not get saved right away, you are getting your prayers answered. Your intercession makes a difference and salvages them before it saves them. Folks, if God does not keep them alive, they are not going to get saved. Your primary goal in prayer ought to be to see them saved, but God may use that very prayer to keep them alive for another day, to bring them through another accident, another situation, to give them one more opportunity.

My dad and I used to pray together often after I got saved. I never heard him pray one time when he did not pray for his brothers to be saved. During his lifetime he saw a couple of them saved. I recall my uncle Donny, who was a drunkard. He had wasted his whole life. He never owned a home. He always ran junk cars. He never had anything. He wore ragged clothes. He spent all his money on booze. He never kept a marriage together. His whole life was in shambles. His health was spent.

I guess I had witnessed to him a dozen times. My dad had witnessed to him many times also. But my dad never failed to pray for my uncle Donny. Uncle Donny went to the hospital. I was out in revival. He had sclerosis of the liver already and he was all bloated up. They would take him in and drain him every so often and help him get back on his feet for a little while and then he would do it again.

My dad went over to see him in the hospital every evening. He took his Bible and sat down and read him some Scripture. He prayed for him every day and every evening while he was with him. After four nights, my dad said to him, "Donny, you know, you are not getting any younger. You know you need to get saved. I have told you many times." My uncle Donny looked up at him with a tear wandering down his cheek and he said, "I know that, Arnie. I am going to do that tonight. I have been waiting for you to come."

He had been run over by cars several times while lying somewhere drunk and passed out. One time he got his whole stomach burned off. They had to graft skin from everywhere to put his stomach back on him. He nearly died that time. He would pass out drunk on the sidewalk, or sleep in his car in sub-zero weather. But I believe God salvaged him and kept him alive because somebody faithfully and effectually prayed and made a difference. *"The effectual fervent prayer of a righteous man availeth much."* Those prayers salvaged him and then finally saved him. I realize it is the Lord Jesus that does the saving, but God says that we are to pray for all men because He wants to save all men. And that means, folks, God is giving a direct correlation between my prayers and their salvation.

I had a revival meeting not long after I went into evangelism. I think we had one hundred and thirty people saved and over seventy baptized. It was an amazing week. One woman came to me on the second night of the meeting and said, "Brother Corle, would you pray for my brothers? My brothers are lost." I said, "I will if you will. Here is what we will do. Let's you, me, and the pastor covenant together to fast and pray, and not eat anything this week until God saves them. Give me their names and I will pray for them. Will you fast with me?" She and the pastor both agreed to fast and pray.

We prayed for them by name, begging God to save them. Two nights later I looked out and one of those brothers was sitting out there. I preached and then gave the invitation. The conviction was evident, but he did not come at first. A few minutes later he stepped out and came down the aisle and fell on the altar, just sobbing and weeping. Somebody dealt with him, he received Christ, and the whole crowd went crazy.

Real revival scares most independent Baptists. If

you have real revival and somebody shouts, if somebody runs down the aisle and hugs their loved one who just got born again, and if a half dozen of them are shouting, it would scare most Baptists to death. That is what revival is like. Revival is not confusion, but when revival breaks out, it brings the joy of God to the hearts of His people, their prayers are answered, their loved ones are saved, the power of God is evident, and there is rejoicing and shouting and praising. We do not know much about real revival.

Revival broke out that night. But she had some brothers still lost. We prayed for the other ones for a couple more days. I looked out on Thursday night, and another brother was sitting there beside his little daughter. I preached and gave the invitation. Others responded and got saved. He was standing back there just fighting it. All of a sudden that little girl looked up at him and tugged on his finger. She said, "Daddy, won't you please get saved?" He stepped out and just staggered down the aisle. He looked like he was fighting a sand storm. He had his hands in front of his face sobbing. He fell on the altar. Somebody dealt with him and he gave his heart to Christ.

There was another brother. Everybody thought he was saved. He was getting ready to go off to Bible college. He was not even in the service that night when his brother got saved. He called the pastor the next day and said, "Would you and Brother Corle come to my house? I want to talk to you." We went over to his house. He said, "I just thought I would tell you. Last night at work, I got on my knees and gave my heart to Christ. I was not saved." I said, "Did you talk to your brother?" He said, "No." I said, "Did you talk to any of the folks down at church?" He said, "No." I said, "That is amazing. God answers prayer."

All three of those brothers got saved. Two of them she knew was lost and one she did not know was lost. But it happened because three people covenanted together and began to fast and pray and beg God to save somebody. Praying for the lost makes a difference.

I am not trying to scold anybody, but you know it is true. The honest truth is the average Christian has not spent five minutes praying for anybody who is lost today. We do not spend five minutes a week praying for lost sinners to be saved, and begging God and interceding for them and praying for their souls.

"Oh, God, give me this. Oh, God, give me that. Oh, God, make this easy. Oh, God, make the load light." What about these poor sinners who are dying and going to hell that do not have anyone on earth who cares enough to pray for them? What about those that are in the same shape as John Newton's friends? What about those who were swept overboard by the waves and perished at sea, when he was salvaged? What about those poor, wretched souls who have no one to intercede for them, no one to pay the price, no one to make up the hedge and stand in the gap? They do not have a Moses. They do not have an Abraham. They do not have a mother or father or anybody that cares enough to intercede, and stand in the gap and make up the hedge. People are dying and going to hell that could be reached.

God said our prayers avail much. I just wonder how many people could have been saved if God's people had learned to pray. I wonder how many people are burning in hell right now that maybe would have lived another ten days if somebody would have prayed for them. I wonder how many are in hell right now that could have been and would have been saved if they had just had one intercessor.

There are people perishing all around us who have

not had anybody pray for them today. We wait until they die and go to hell and then we worry about it. Why don't you worry about it before they die? If you pray, maybe God will keep them alive a little longer. Maybe God will get the Gospel to them one more time. Maybe they will repent and be saved. God said He wants us to pray for all men for He would have all men to be saved. Our prayers avail much. They make a difference.

You need to make a prayer project of somebody today. You need to get a list of people that you want to see saved. I do not care if they are wicked people or nice people, people you love, people you hate. It does not take great preaching to get people saved, it takes somebody in the prayer closet interceding for their soul. God wants to save them, but He said it is dependent on whether or not you pray for all men, then He can save all men.

We do not want that much responsibility, do we? We have it anyway, whether we want it or not, and we had better learn to pray. We are going to face God one of these days, not only over our soulwinning, not only over our church attendance, not only over our giving, but over our prayer lives, and if God would have us to pray for all men, and intercede for all men, we had better get busy doing it.

If you are saved, you are the answer to somebody's prayers. Somebody prayed for you. Somebody begged God for your soul. I wonder if they had been as fruitless and careless in their prayer life as you are in yours if you would have ever been saved. I wonder if they had been as inconsistent as we are if we would be saved. I wonder if they would have been so haphazard that they did not even write our names down and pray over us if we would ever have been saved.

Will you be the pray-er that saves somebody's soul as the answer to your prayers? People die and go to hell that maybe could have lived long enough to get saved if they had an intercessor. You say, "Well I do not think it is that big a deal." I know. That is why you do not do it. The reason is because you want to appease your conscience. If it is no big deal, then it is no big deal if you do not do it, is it? We can always blame it on the signs of the times, and this dispensation, but people are not being reached. It is not because we are in some church period, it is because we are in a time of prayerlessness. We go through the carnal motions of soulwinning, and we have not even prayed.

God help us to learn to pray for the lost. He said in our text, *"I exhort therefore, that, first of all,"* when? "first of all," get this thing done first! *"first of all, supplications, prayers, intercessions, and giving of thanks, be made for all men;...For this is good and acceptable in the sight of God...Who will have all men to be saved, and come unto the knowledge of the truth."* I had better learn to pray. Somebody is going to die and go to hell if we do not learn to pray. Somebody you love could be salvaged if you would do what John Newton's mother did. There is some wicked young man that would be saved if you would do what my mother and dad did. There is some wicked young man that would be salvaged if you would do what Joe Boyd's mother did. There are some wicked, ungodly people that deserve judgment that would have one more chance to repent if you would do what Moses did. There are some folks who would be salvaged if you would do what Abraham did.

If we do not snap out of our prayerlessness we are going to have more to account for at the judgment seat of Christ than you ever imagined. God ought to break our hearts today over our prayerlessness. If you do not think what I am saying is true, you just have your normal prayer time tonight. Pop the tape recorder on and pray like you always pray. Rewind it and listen to it. You will be able to figure out why our country is in the shape that it is in.

We are the elite - the saved, separated, independent Baptist, soulwinning church. We are the ones with the convictions and the standards. In spite of all that, we are a prayerless people. And when we do pray, we are so selfish. God help us to get serious about this business of praying for the lost. God would have you to pray for all men because He would have all men to be saved. Your effectual fervent prayer will avail much. As Samuel said, "God forbid that you should sin against the Lord in ceasing to pray" for the lost.

CHAPTER THIRTEEN

PRAYERLESS PRAYING

"Therefore I say unto you, What things soever ye desire, when ye pray, believe that ye receive them, and ye shall have them." (Mark 11:24)

Most preaching on Mark 11:24 deals with the subject of faith. But this text also deals with something that is a real problem, Prayerless Praying. There are three elements mentioned that have to do with real prayer. The first is the desire, then the request, and finally the faith. If all three of those elements are not involved, it is prayerless praying. Most of the time, the thing that we emphasize is faith. We make people think they have to have some kind of real strong, supernatural faith to get an answer to prayer.

In the Book of Acts they were praying for Peter when he was in jail. But when he got out of jail they were shocked. It does not look to me like they had great faith. They did not have enough faith to expect a miracle, but they did have enough faith to ask for one. It is not great faith that gets answers, it is having enough faith to come to God with your need. It is having enough faith to ask for a miracle, whether you think it is going to happen or not.

Some folks just do not pray. They do not make their requests to God. But many folks who do pray do so to no avail.

Desire is a missing ingredient in our prayers. Desire is the very basis of prayer. Jesus did not say, "Whatsoever ye ask when ye pray..." He did not say, "Whatsoever you want when you pray..." He said, *"What things soever ye desire, when ye pray..."* You have to have desire or it is not prayer. Desire is as much an element in prayer as faith is. Desire is as much a true element of prayer as requesting is. I am afraid a lot of times we ask for things we do not really desire in our soul. There is no yearning in our souls, no groaning in our spirit.

The order of prayer is this: first I have a need. We do not like needs, do we? God knows if He did not create needs in your life you would never pray. The first thing God does is allows us to have a need. The second thing that happens is because I have a need, I have a desire. Because I have a desire, I believe that I cannot take care of it but God can. I have faith that God can take care of this need that I have, and I want to be taken care of. Because I think God can take care of it, (that is faith), I make request, I come to God and I ask. Then God sends the answer.

The very premise of prayer, the very basis of prayer, is desire. It is missing from most prayers that are prayed. Many of us go through the motions of prayer. We go through the formality. We mouth words to God with no desire in our souls, with no hungering in our hearts, with no yearning in our souls. We are not really praying. We are going through the motions of prayer. It is only the shell, the outward show of prayer.

In Isaiah 58:2 God describes that kind of praying. He said, *"Yet they seek me daily, and delight to know my ways, as a nation that did righteousness, and forsook not the ordinance of their God: they ask of me the ordinances of justice; they take delight in approaching to God."* He said, "They want to know My ways." They would not put up with a guy who did not preach the truth. Now, they are not going to live it, but they would not put up with a guy who did not preach it. God said, "They get excited about their approach to God, but they have no passion in their prayer. They get excited about going through the motion of prayer. They delight in the practice and the formality of prayer, but they are never changed by it because they have no desire fueling their prayers."

Prayer ought to be part of our spiritual habit. But when prayer becomes habit only, when it becomes duty only, it ceases to be prayer. God wants us to understand that prayer is more than just going through a motion. Prayer is more than mouthing some words, more than a formality. Prayer is not a petition, it is a passion. It is not just a habit, it is something that is driven from the soul of a person because of a hunger for something that God can give.

In I John 5:15 the Bible says, *"If we know that he hear us, whatsoever we ask, we know that we have the petitions that we desired of him."* The Bible says I do not get everything I ask for. I may make ten requests, but I am going to get what I really desire, what I really yearn for. I am afraid a lot of times we spend ten minutes, fifteen minutes, twenty minutes mouthing words to God that we do not really have any passion behind. There is no driving force. There is nothing burning in our soul. There is no yearning in our heart, and because of that we have done some prayerless praying. One of the great elements of prayer was missing, the element of desire, the very basis of prayer.

In Matthew 18:32 the Bible says, *"Then his lord, after that he had called him, said unto him, O thou wicked servant, I forgave thee all that debt, because thou desiredst me."* That means that you could ask God to forgive you, you can read a list of your sins to God with no remorse, no repentance in your soul, no real desire to be forgiven and cleansed and changed, mouth the words and not get forgiveness. We can pray prayers and they will be nothing more than a meaningless formality. It will be prayerless praying. No reality to it, and no answer.

James 5:16 says, *"The effectual fervent prayer of a righteous man availeth much."* That word 'fervent' means 'to be stretched out.' It speaks of a runner in the finishing kick of a race, on the last lap, the last yardage, when he is heading into the finish line. He is straining every muscle. That is what fervency speaks of. It also speaks of something being boiling hot, something boiling in the soul of a person.

That means if there is no desire, no passion, no heat, no fervor, there is no real prayer and it does not avail. Prayer with no fervor does not make a difference. It does not receive answers.

One of the great secrets of our lack of answered prayer can be found in the weakness of our desires. We have become so content in this society. What is destroying us is not necessarily the presence of evil desire, but the absence of godly desire. There is something lacking, something missing, that desperately needs to be found again.

Prayerless praying does not produce answers, nor does it produce believers. It produces atheists and infidels. Charles G. Finney, as a young man, still lost, had a church ask him, "Would you like us to pray for you?" He said, "No, I really would not. You pray all the time, and you never get any answers to prayer." He could not figure out if these people were not really believers, and therefore could not get an answer, or if he misunderstood the promises of the Bible, or if there really was no God. It nearly drove him to the brink of skepticism.

Prayerless praying, going through the motions again and again and again with no answer and nothing changing is not going to do much for your faith. It is not going to do much for anybody that knows you are praying. God does answer prayer.

Desire is said to be the will in action. Desire has concentration and fire. It wants a few things and wants them badly. It is not scrambled with ten thousand thoughts. Desire is narrow and single-minded, and there is something it must have.

Most people's prayers have no intensity or fervency. They are not stretched out, laboring in prayer.

Strong desire makes for strong prayers. Desire goes after those things it wants with everything that it has. It is desire that arms prayer with a thousand pleas and robes it with invincible courage so that it will not be denied. It provides determination. Desire is the basis of determination as well.

As I travel around the country I am finding that fundamentalism has all the mechanical looks of real Christianity, but it lacks the fervent heat of desire and passion in the depths of its soul. There is no passion in prayer and there is no passion in soulwinning. We have prayerless praying and preachless preaching and soulless soulwinning.

We keep the form while the inner life fades and dies and the heart grows cold and indifferent and literally unconcerned. We delight in approaching to God. We think we are good Christians because we set a time aside and say a few words of prayer. But we have no passion. You ask for things you do not even want. You ask for things that would be an imposition on your lifestyle if you got them.

The boiling heat of fervent prayer has been tempered to a respectable lukewarmness. Lukewarmness makes God sick. God never intended for us to be lukewarm. He said, "If you are not going to be red hot, I would rather you were ice cold than lukewarm."

That passage used to puzzle me. I used to wonder, "Now, lukewarm is closer to hot than cold is. If God really wants me red hot, why would He not rather have me lukewarm than cold?" Then it dawned on me that hot is uncomfortable. Cold is uncomfortable. Lukewarm is comfortable. If you get it hot enough, it will burn out the impurities. If you get it cold enough, it will freeze out the impurities. Every disease thrives in that warm, damp, dark place of lukewarmness. God said, "I want you red hot, but if you are not going to be red hot, I would rather you were as cold as an ice cube so you get convicted so badly that you are uncomfortable, so that it freezes out any excitement or fun that you would have in sin, so that it destroys the very germ that would be the destruction of you."

Prayerless praying lacks the essential elements of true prayer. True prayer is based on desire. It has earnestness involved in it. Most people's prayers have no reckless abandon like the prayers of those in the Bible, or like great revivalists of days gone by.

In Exodus chapter thirty-two Moses came down the mountain from God. God said, "The people have given themselves to idolatry. Step back, Moses. I am going to kill them all and start over with you." Moses, with a quivering voice, fell to his face and said, "Oh, God, please deliver them, and if not, blot me out of Thy book also." He said, "If You are going to kill them, go ahead and kill me." It sounds to me like there may have been some desire in that prayer. It sounds to me like there was a little bit of reckless abandon involved in that prayer. It sounds to me like there was some passion in that prayer. It sounds to me like there was something that Moses wanted, and he wanted it badly. He wanted God to deliver those people. He wanted God to withhold His hand of judgment. He prayed and put himself on the line.

We do not have much of that reckless abandon like Jacob had in Peniel when he said, *"I will not let thee go, except thou bless me."* He was not talking to a man. He was talking to God. He said, "I am holding onto You and I am not letting go until I get the blessing." By the way, it cost him too. The sinew in the hollow of his thigh was shrunk. He limped for the rest of his life. He did not mind the price he had to pay because he said, "There is something I have to have." He came out of that a prince with God and with man. He had prevailed. There is such a thing as prevailing prayer. It is prayer with great desire. It is prayer with great heat and fervency. It is prayer with a determination to importune until the answer comes. The reason you pray once and quit is because you have no desire. The reason you mouth prayers and do not know what you said fifteen minutes later is because you did not pray with any fervent desire. It is not something that burns in your soul. It is not something you want.

Some of you have been praying for revival and you do not want one. You have been praying for sinners to be saved, but you could not care less in the depths of your soul. There is no passion burning in your heart. There is no fervent desire in your soul. There is no driving force in your prayers. Your prayer time is a cumbersome time. It is not a time of force and passion. It is not a time of coming to God with great desire and great fervency. That is why you pray five minutes and think you have prayed an hour.

Paul said, *"I could wish myself accursed from Christ for my brethren, my kinsmen according to the flesh."* That was his desire and his request. He said, "Oh, God, if it were possible, I would be willing to go to hell to see these Jews get saved." Do you think if you would be willing to go to hell you might be willing to walk across the street and knock on a door or two? Do you think if you would be willing to go to hell to see them saved you might be willing to schedule some time for soulwinning every week? Paul was not blowing smoke. Paul was consistent in his soulwinning. He labored day and night because something burned in the depths of his soul. He prayed with reckless abandon. "God, I would be willing to go to hell to see people saved." It was evident that it was real and it was not some facade. He was not mouthing words that were impressive.

By the way, God put those words into the Bible. That pretty well tells me it was the desire of Paul's heart or God would have never printed it in His Book. He had a passion burning inside of him. He said, "I want them to be saved. I pray for them to be saved. I would give my life to see them saved. I would be willing to go to hell to see them saved." It sounds to me like he had some desire. It sounds to me like there was some reckless abandon. It sounds to me like there was something he wanted and wanted badly. That is what real prayer is.

There are some Christians who have never prayed a genuine prayer since they have been saved. There has not been anything they have wanted badly. There has not been anything they have begged God for, that their heart and soul have burned for. It is kind of casual. "I can live with it or without it." "Lord, I would like this, and if You would provide it, it would be wonderful. If not, I will miss church for two weeks and work overtime and get it for myself."

The Bible tells us about that Syrophenician woman. She wanted her daughter healed. Jesus said, "It is not meet to give the children's bread to dogs." She said, "Yes, Lord, but even the dogs eat of the crumbs that fall from their master's table." She said, "I do not care if I get the answer as a dog or a person, I have to have it." Her pride did not get in the way. Her desire outweighed her pride. That is more than most of us could say. If somebody says something to upset you, your pride outweighs everything. It outweighs your reasoning power, it outweighs your Bible principles, it outweighs your element of forgiveness.

That woman said, "There is something I have to have. Something burns in my soul. I have a daughter who has a great need. Jesus, You can meet that need and I am asking You to meet that need. This is not a formality with me. This is not the hollow shell. I have to have it."

Jacob said, "I need the blessing of God. It burns in my soul. Whatever it costs I have to have it. I am not just delighting in approaching to You. I am not just delighting in the formality. I am not just delighting in the outward show. There is something that burns in my soul. I have to have it."

David said, *"As the hart panteth after the water brooks, so panteth my soul after thee, O God."* He said, "I am hard after the heart of God. I am hard after communion with God. There is something I desire." In Psalm 27:4 he said, *"One thing have I desired of the LORD, that will I seek after; that I may dwell in the house of the LORD all the days of my life, to behold the beauty of the LORD, and to inquire in his temple."*

He said, "There is a driving force in my life. It is the force in my prayer, but it is the force in my daily living too."

John Knox said, "Oh, God, give me Scotland or I die." David Brainerd said, "Give me souls, or take my soul." It sounds to me like there was some passion in their soul. Everybody who was ever known as a great man of prayer prayed with reckless abandon. They prayed with a passion, a heat, a fervency. They did not pray flowery prayers. They did not pray pretty prayers. They prayed with passion burning in their soul, begging God for something. They said, "I have to have it."

These statements indicate strong and earnest desire. In Proverbs 10:24 the Bible says, *"The desire of the righteous shall be granted."* The request? No, the desire. In Psalm 10:17 the Bible says, *"LORD, thou hast heard the desire of the humble."* That means God hears everything I desire. Not everything I ask for. Not everything I request. Not everything I mechanically write down and read off to God. He hears what I desire.

Most of us prayed this morning but God did not hear a thing. Why? Because He hears and gives us the things that we desire. *'We know we have the petitions that we desired of him."*

The Bible tells us God will give us right desires. In Psalm 37:4 the Bible says, *"Delight thyself also in the LORD; and he shall give thee the desires of thine heart."* Just about everybody who preaches that says, "Now, if you will just delight yourself in the Lord, He will give you anything you want." That is not what it says. That is not what it means either. I will prove it with another verse later. What the Bible says is, if I will delight myself in the Lord, and He is my delight, and He is the object of my love, and He is the desire of my heart, if I delight myself in Him, He will give me my desires. If I delight myself in Him He will give me desires in my heart that I ought to have. It does not mean I just say, "I delight in You, Lord, now here is what I really want."

If I delight in Him, He will put good desires in my heart. When He puts the desire in there, and I yearn with the desire God put into my heart, He can honor that desire. He can answer that prayer. If God gives me my desire it means my desire was born in the heart of God instead of in my heart. If I delight in Him, and He gives me the desire I ought to have that is His heart's desire, if I pray according to His desire, He can give me the answer. Psalm 85:6 says, *"Wilt thou not revive us again, that thy people may rejoice in thee?"*

God put a desire in Solomon's heart for wisdom. Solomon asked God for wisdom. God said, "Because you did not ask the life of your enemies, and you did not ask for great wealth and power, I am going to give you wisdom to take care of My people, and I am also going to give you everything you did not ask for." That is pretty good. Why did he get all that? Because God gave him his desire and he prayed according to that desire, with that passion burning in his soul, and God said, "I can honor that. I can do something with that."

In II Chronicles 15:15 the Bible says, *"And all Judah rejoiced at the oath: for they had sworn with all their heart, and sought him with their whole desire; and he was found of them."* Why was He found? Because they sought Him with all their heart and with all their desire, *"and the LORD gave them rest round about."*

In Isaiah 26:9 the Bible says, *"With my soul have I desired thee... yeah, with my spirit within me will I seek thee early."* He said, "My desire is for You, God. My yearning is for You, Oh God. I want You. I want to know You. I yearn after You." God met with him and answered that request and gave him desires for other things.

In Psalm 21:1-2 the Bible says, *"The king shall joy in thy strength, O LORD; and in thy salvation how greatly shall he rejoice! Thou hast given him his heart's desire, and hast not withholden the request of his lips."* It sounds like God answered his prayers too. Do you know what David did? He got consumed with God. He got wrapped up with the person of God. He fell in love with God. He was delighting in God, in God's strength and God's glory. When he did that, God gave him his desires. When God gave him his desires, David prayed according to the desires that God put into his heart, and God did not withhold the requests of David's lips. God answered his prayers.

Most of our desires come from the world, from the flesh, and from the devil. Most of the things we come to the prayer closet with were not even born in the heart of God. They have nothing to do with the glory of God. We are not consumed with the person of God. As a matter of fact, most of us have to squeeze God into our schedules. If God is going to get any of your time, it is going to be extra, left over minutes and you will squeeze Him in. He does not have preeminence. He does not have first place. Your mind and heart are not consumed with Him.

Psalm 145:18-19 says, *"The LORD is nigh unto all them that call upon him, to all that call upon him in truth. He will fulfill the desire of them that fear him: he also will hear their cry, and will save them."* God will honor their desire. He will meet their needs. He is going to answer their prayer.

We are doing a tremendous amount of prayerless praying. We delight to approach unto God. We delight in the habit. We delight in the formality. But one of the great elements, the very basis of prayer, the matter of desire, is missing in our prayer time. It is missing in our requests.

The basis of real prayer is desire. Formality will be consumed by desire. Faith will be enflamed by desire. Deadness with be transformed into a dynamo of power when it is driven by desire. Cumbersome duty becomes a consecrated delight in the prayer closet when there is desire that drives me to my knees and desire that drives the requests from my lips and desire that fuels my prayer life.

Prayerless praying is neither powerful, nor is it palatable. It is not even something that people can bear for very long. A lot of people have quit praying all together because they are convinced prayer does not work. Real prayer does work, but prayerless praying does not work. Prayerless praying will make prayerless people in time. You will get to the place where you do not even delight in going through the formality anymore. All of a sudden you will realize it is just a formality.

There are many, many Christians who have not prayed in a long, long time. There was a time when you did a bunch of prayerless praying with no passion and no driving force. You delighted in approaching unto God. One day it dawned on you, "I am doing nothing but going through a formality. This is not real, and it does not work for me. Nothing is happening. I may as well quit." Now you do not even go through the motion of prayer. Now you do not even practice the duty of prayer. Now you do not even delight in approaching unto God.

Our prayers give formal utterance to things for which our hearts are not only not hungry, but for things for which our hearts do not even have an appetite. Let me illustrate what I am saying. We pray for God to stem the tide of evil. Then we live in such a way as to encourage evil and wickedness. We pray for humility and then nurture pride. We pray for self-denial, and then indulge the flesh. We pray for souls, then will not even go soulwinning. We pray for souls, and will not make a phone call. We pray for souls, and will not get involved in anything that would bring one to Jesus Christ. We pray for revival and then live in such a way as to stifle any hope of revival. We live in sin and selfishness and pride and dishonesty. We say, "Oh, God, send revival." Then we get up off of our knees and live in such a way that we know we will kill any hope of revival.

You go ahead and delight in the formality but God says it will avail nothing. It is *"the effectual fervent prayer of a righteous man"* that availeth much. *"Whatsoever ye desire when ye pray..."* *"I forgave thee all that debt because thou desiresdt me."* *"We have the petitions that we desired of him."* God will answer the desire of the righteous.

Most of you, if you pray, fifteen minutes after you pray you do not remember what you prayed about. You get together at a prayer meeting and you pray, and fifteen minutes after the prayer meeting, if you had to tell anybody what you prayed about, for the most part you would have no idea. Do you know why? Because it was not born in desire. It was not something that burned in our soul. It was just a formal utterance. It was something that sounded good to the brethren. It was something that filled up the time slot that we had designated. It was something that we delighted in doing because it was religious activity. But we do not even remember what we prayed for because it was not burning in our soul.

If there is something you really want, you will not forget what you were praying about. If there is something that burns as a passion in your soul, fifteen minutes later it still burns. Fifteen minutes later it is still evident. Fifteen minutes later it is still real to you. You still want it. You will not haphazardly forget what you prayed about because it is born in desire. Desire indelibly prints the object of the desire on the soul.

The Bible talks about the Lord Jesus and how He prayed with a great passion. In Hebrews chapter five it says that He prayed with strong crying. He lifted up His voice and wept with strong crying. There was something

He desired.

Praying Hyde's prayer life was unbelievable. It is said that he prayed with such great intensity that his heart literally moved from one side of his chest to the other. He lost himself in his prayers. He forgot time. He forgot his surroundings. He forgot everything else. He was consumed with a desire. A passion burned in his soul.

David Brainerd, on one occasion, prayed out in the open air in about two feet of snow. He got on his knees, praying for the American Indians. He lost track of time. He prayed with such intensity that he melted snow down to the ground in a six foot circle around his body in the open air. Most of us do not have enough passion in our prayers to melt an ice cube in a seventy degree room with our prayers.

No wonder David Brainerd could preach to the Indians through a drunken interpreter and get thousands of people saved. No wonder God could use him in such a marvelous way to overcome the language barrier of the people he so desired to reach. Most of the preaching he ever did he did in his own language, hoping that God would do something in the Indians' hearts, or he did it through a drunken interpreter. People were saved by the score. Why? Because he knew something about fervent prayer. He did not indulge in an empty formality. He did not indulge in prayerless praying. He did not just delight in approaching, he delighted in fervency and in getting a hold of God.

My girls want everything they see. They ask for things. They say, "Dad, how about one of those? Could we get one of those?" "Dad, could we have one of these? Dad, how about one of those?" It is a passing fancy when they see something. I say, "Well, no." That is the last I hear about it.

But when my girls find something that is not wrong to have, and they convince me they really want it, when they get to where they want it badly, they get it just about every time. I do not get them every little thing they want. I do not get them every little thing they ask for. But there are some things through the years that they wanted and wanted badly, and when I knew they wanted it badly, they got it. They did not get it because they asked for it. They did not get it because it was a passing fancy. They got it because they really wanted it.

God is a lot better Father than I am. When He puts the right desire in our hearts and we really, really want something that is good to have, God will give us what we desire.

We have three crowds of people in our Baptist churches. (1) We have folks who do not even pray. You do not even go through the formality. You do not even delight in approaching unto God. There are people reading this who have not even gone through the motion of prayer in a month. You may bow your head and breathe a prayer at meal time. But it is formality. As far as having a set time and a set place and a prayer list and actually going through the formality of prayer, you do not even do that.

(2) Some of you do have a set time and you do have a list, and pretty regularly you delight in approaching unto God. But it is casual. You say, "Dad, could we have one of those? Dad, I would like one of those. Boy, isn't that nice? Could we have one of those?" But you have not come to the place where you say, "Oh, I have to have it. I have to have it."

(3) There may be somebody who understands what I am talking about. If there are some, there are not many. Prayer must be a fervent desire. Prayer must be more than a religious activity. Prayer is a passion, not a

performance. It there is no passion, there is no prayer. There is just a hollow motion.

If I took a huge cannon ball and set it down in front of your church, and rolled it slowly toward the back of the auditorium, that huge cannon ball would probably not move anybody at all. You would sit there glibly and watch. You would say, "Huh, isn't that something?" It is a big cannon ball, but there is no force behind it. There is no power behind it.

But if I took a .45 caliber muzzle loader and I put a .45 caliber ball in there with a charge of powder, and I pointed it out over the crowd and squeezed the trigger, I guarantee you everybody in the building would move. Why? Because of the size of the ball? No, because of the force behind it.

It is not the size of the prayer, it is the force behind it that makes things happen. One of the lacking elements in our prayer lives is the element of desire. Desire is the very basis of prayer. That means if there is no desire, you did not pray. You just delighted in the formality. You did not get an answer. You did not move the heart of God because there was nothing you really wanted. There was no force. No fire.

God help us to repent of our lack of desire.

I am more frustrated about lack of desire than I am anything that I know of. That is why some of you sit in church looking bored stiff. There is nothing you really want. You are spoiled rotten. The devil has given you a shot of novocaine in your "want to." You are satisfied and you are as sorry as a snake. You are content. The world is going to hell and the church is not doing all that it ought to be doing.

I can tell you how to have revival, but I cannot make you want one. I can tell you how to get your prayers answered, but I cannot make you want anything.

I can tell you how to win a soul, but I cannot make you want to.

In the last year, I have written and preached more sermons on the subject of desire than any other subject. I think that is where everything begins. I know that is where prayer begins. I have a Bible verse on that.

Proverbs 18:1 says desire is where separation begins too. That is where soulwinning begins. It is something that is missing today. If you are going to go through the motions, you may as well go ahead and get something to fuel it, passion, desire in your soul, something you really want. Pray with fervency.

CHAPTER FOURTEEN

PRAY WITHOUT CEASING
(I Thessalonians 5:17)

The first verse that our daughter Lydia memorized was I Thessalonians 5:17, *"Pray without ceasing."* The first verse that our daughter Rebekah learned when she was old enough to talk and memorize a verse was I Thessalonians 5:17. Many of you have committed that verse to memory. You have rejoiced as your children have memorized the verse, yet I believe there is something in this verse that you and I have failed to practice. There is something we have failed to put into daily life. *"Pray without ceasing."*

Does that mean that the only thing I do is pray? The first time I read the verse it puzzled me. I thought to myself, "How in the world could you pray without ceasing? You mean, you do not sleep? you do not work? you do not do anything else?" God is not talking about us not doing anything but praying. God wants us to get Him on the line in the morning, and then shoulder the phone the rest of the day.

Have you ever seen someone in the kitchen cooking with the phone on their shoulder? Have you ever seen someone in the shop working with the phone on their shoulder? What are they doing? They do not have to stop talking to somebody on the telephone to work, and they do not have to stop working to talk. God wants you to understand that to "pray without ceasing" means that I get my call in to heaven in the morning, I get in touch with heaven in the morning, and then I shoulder the phone the rest of the day. When I finish my morning prayer time, instead of ending it with a period I should end it with a comma or a semicolon. I continue my conversation with God all day long. There is a real problem here, because I cannot continue what I do not start. I cannot maintain what I do not establish. If I do not think that prayer is important enough to schedule it in my morning and to start my day with fellowship with God, I cannot continue through the day what I did not start in the morning. If I never pick the phone up and dial, if I leave it on the cradle and never get a call in to heaven, if I do not get in touch I cannot stay in touch.

You are not going to stay in touch with God through the day if He does not have a prominent place in the morning. It is vital that God's people learn to touch base with heaven first thing in the morning. I am not telling you how long to pray, or what time you have to start. I am simply telling you that you need to start the day with God. If God is not in first place in the morning, He will be in last place all day long. If you do not get the call in in the morning, you will get so busy that you will never get it in.

God wants me to be in constant communion and fellowship with Him. When God created Adam and Eve, their primary purpose for existence was not work. He did give them work to do and work is good for all of us. God's work is exciting and it is good. Work in general is good. It was not part of the curse. They had work before the fall. But their primary purpose for existence was to walk with God in the cool of the day, to have communion with God, to love Him back, to know Him personally and intimately.

I am convinced that the average born again Christian knows nothing about their purpose for existence. They know nothing about a sweet communion and fellowship with God that starts in the morning and continues all day long throughout their waking hours, talking to God about everything all the time. It does not mean that I do nothing but pray, but I maintain a spirit of prayer as I perform my daily activities. Everything I do is seasoned with prayer.

A spirit of prayer is a spirit of revival. But most of us wait until we are in trouble and then call on God. We wait until the trouble starts before we try to find God. We wait until the battle starts. That is a bad time to try and get a hold of God. That is a bad time to have to get a hold of heaven.

Back some time ago when Tom Vineyard was in Zaire, Africa, he took his wife into town to get a check up. She was pregnant at that time. Tom went to another place about a mile from the hospital. He was supposed to call his dad at a certain time on that day. He got on the telephone and called Jim Vineyard, his dad.

While Tom was talking to his dad, Brother Vineyard said he heard a noise on the other end of the line. He said his mind knew what it was, but his heart did not want to believe it. What he thought he heard was machine gun fire. He recognized it from the time he spent in combat.

Tom said to him, "Just a minute, Dad." He lay the phone down and walked away. He came back and picked the telephone up. He said, "Dad, there is a machine gun firing right outside of my window." Brother Vineyard said, "Son, get on your belly. Do not run. Do not be a spectator looking out the window. If you have to go to Melissa, you can crawl a mile on your belly, but do not get up. People who run in wars get shot. Stay down.

"Now, Son, you remember all that stuff your dad taught you about situations like this, don't you?" On the other end of the line there was a long pause. Tom said, "Dad, right now I cannot remember anything."

That is usually the way it is when trouble starts.

The fact that he had his father on the line when the war broke out may have been his salvation. He might have panicked. He might have run. He might have tried to leave the building and get to his wife. He might have made a foolish decision in haste in the midst of all the excitement. He might have made a wrong decision that could have been fatal. But because he had his father on the line when the war started, and his father knew what he needed to do, it salvaged him and kept him from panicking, and making a bad choice.

I do not care what battle takes place in your life or what trouble may come, your Father knows what you ought to do about it. Most of us have been preached to and we know, but in the midst of all the adversity and when the battle begins to rage sometimes, we cannot remember all that we have been taught. Sometimes we do not think our way through. But if we have our Father on the line all day long, when the battle starts we will not get caught by surprise. We will not need to try to get to God like He is a 911 number or a spare tire.

In Luke 18:1 the Bible says that *"...men ought always to pray, and not to faint."* He said two things. (1) *"Men ought always to pray".* That word "always" is a Greek word that means "always." Excuse me for getting so deep. What God is saying is pray all the time, about everything, good and bad. (2) *"and not to faint."* That tells me that if I am not always praying, I will faint. "To faint" means "to give up." Somebody who faints is not hit on the head with a club and knocked out. They give up consciousness. God says that if I do not pray and keep in touch with heaven, I am going to get discouraged by the circumstances and give up. I am going to throw in the towel.

When I talk about always praying, that means at work, and that means at home.

Ladies have some of the most cumbersome work that people can have. I mean washing dishes, running the vacuum cleaner, and all that stuff you have to do every day. Then your husband comes home and messes it all up. You say, "How do you know?" Because I am a husband. Then you have to get out of bed tomorrow and do the same thing you did today.

Those times do not have to be monotonous times. Those things that seem to be dreary and cumbersome can become a blessing, if while you run the vacuum cleaner and while you stand at the sink, you spend your time in communion with God. I imagine if you can talk on the phone while you are doing the dishes you could talk to God while you are doing that, too. I imagine if you can talk on the phone while you are ironing and doing other things, you could probably talk to God when you do not even have to handle the phone receiver.

Fellowship with God is never cumbersome. Fellowship with God is never dreary. I can take those moments that get wasted while I am doing the duties of the day and commune with God while I am working, and while I am cleaning, and while I am doing the things I am supposed to do.

You men who have to drive an hour to work, instead of cussing everybody you could go ahead and fellowship with God. Instead of getting frustrated when you are caught in traffic, and having down time, wasted time, lost time, time that escapes you, it can be time that is profitable for your spiritual growth and your walk with God. You can have fellowship with God when you are stranded on the freeway and while you are driving down the highway.

While you are serving God and soulwinning you can be praying. God wants you to learn to have everything seasoned with prayer. God wants us to have seasons of prayer when we do nothing but pray. We need to get to a secluded place, on purpose, at a scheduled time, with a prayer list, get on our knees and do nothing but pray and talk to God.

Many of us do not even have a prayer time. That is a tragedy. But many of us who do have a prayer time do it like this: We get out of bed in the morning, we have our schedule, we do our duty, and we go through our routine. We have our time of prayer, and as soon as we say "Amen" we forget about God until tomorrow morning. We do not speak another word to Him until tomorrow morning unless we get into trouble.

God wants us to have a good habit. He wants us to schedule time to spend with Him, but when you get through your list, do not hang up on Him, shoulder the phone. The rest of the day stay in touch with God.

When I was traveling with Joe Boyd I discovered that he prayed about everything. He is a man of prayer. He would say to me, "Son, let's pray." "Son, let's pray." "Son, let's pray." It did not matter what we were doing. He engrained that into me. If something broke, we prayed. If something was going good we prayed. If he got lost, which was about three times a day, we prayed.

In Ephesians 6:18 the Bible says, *"praying always,"* all the time, about everything. Philippians 4:6 says, *"Be careful for nothing; but in every thing by prayer and supplication with thanksgiving let your requests be made known unto God."* He said, "Be careful for nothing." That word "careful" comes from a root word that means "to tear with hooks." God is saying, "Be torn up about nothing, but pray about everything."

You are going to have some circumstances to deal with. You will either be torn up or you will pray. You can sit around and pout and get a bad spirit. You can let all kinds of things bother you and destroy your joy and keep you from enjoying life, or you can pray about everything instead of allowing yourself to be torn up and shredded by every problem that comes into your life. Praying without ceasing keeps me in a position where I do not have to be torn up if I talk to God about everything.

Stonewall Jackson, a great general, was killed by accident by his own snipers. He was probably the greatest strategist involved in the war at that time. If, in God's providence, he had not been killed in such a manner, the war may have turned out differently.

He was a great man of prayer, a very godly man. He made this statement. "I have so fixed the habit of prayer in my mind that I never raise a glass of water to my lips without asking God's blessing. I never seal a letter without putting a word of prayer under the seal. I never take a letter from the post without sending a brief thought heavenward. I never change classes in the lecture room without praying for the cadets who go out and the cadets who come in."

If I understand what he was expressing, he was simply saying, "I have so fixed the habit of prayer in my mind, that I pray about everything." He did not wait until trouble came. He prayed about everything. He did not wait until he was torn up. He was prayed up before the problem came. He continued in a spirit of prayer. He had learned well what it meant to pray without ceasing. Everything in his life was seasoned by prayer. All of his labor was seasoned by prayer.

The old timers used to call this kind of praying "ejaculatory prayer." That comes from a Latin word that means "to shoot a dart." It was a war time word. God says that this kind of prayer is where I swiftly shoot a dart of prayer off to heaven without any preparation. Ejaculatory prayer is spontaneous prayer. It is extemporaneous prayer. Unplanned, unwritten, unscheduled, where God moves in my heart about something and I pray while I am doing what I am doing. It just flows forth from my heart and I shoot a prayer to heaven. It is not the length that makes it prayer.

David Brainerd quite frequently said, "I spent much time in ejaculatory prayer this morning." All morning long God was moving in his heart, and he was shooting prayers to heaven, one after another, to the throne of God.

God wants us to get to the place where prayer is as natural as breathing, where prayer is a spontaneous action, where prayer just flows forth unplanned, where He can move our heart and we labor and pray while we drive and pray while we work, and pray while we serve. We just continually, as God moves our heart, shoot prayers off to heaven. We make a difference all day long.

It is said of Billy Sunday that he would walk down the street and talk a little bit to Ma Sunday and then he would talk a little bit to Jesus. He would talk a little bit to Ma Sunday and then he would talk a little bit to Jesus. To Billy Sunday, Jesus was as real as Ma Sunday was. I imagine he was kind of strange. He was peculiar. The Bible does say we are supposed to be peculiar people. The primary thought is not that we are to look funny. But it is peculiar to a lost world for you to talk to somebody that they cannot see, for you to talk to somebody that they do not even believe is there.

Most of us do not do it because we do not think He is there either. We feel awkward because it is like we are talking to ourselves or talking into the air, talking to somebody who is not there. It would be a wonderful thing if God's people ever really believed He was ever present like He promised to be. *"Lo, I am with you alway."* It would be wonderful if we ever got a hold of the fact that He wants to hear from us all day long and for us to stay in constant fellowship and communion. Billy Sunday talked to God like He was real. Do you?

There was no formality to this kind of praying. It was conversation. It was communion. He never allowed his communion with God to get cold. He never allowed the conversation with God to be over for the day. In his waking hours he kept in contact.

Charles Spurgeon said in his latter years that he made it a habit never to let a thirty minute period pass without talking to his God. He did it on purpose until it became a habit.

Something that is a habit is something that you do without thinking. When I smoked cigarettes, I did not have to think about reaching for a cigarette. It was reflex action. I woke up in the morning reaching for the nightstand to get a hold of those cigarettes. The first thing I would do is sit up in bed and get my fix. Some of you know what I am talking about. I had developed a habit. I had become addicted to something. I had done it when it did not taste good and I did not like it until it became a reflex action, a habitual action, a spontaneous action. That is what Spurgeon said he did.

John Hyde was known as "Praying Hyde," "The Apostle of Prayer," and some called him "the man who never sleeps," because of his constant communion day and night with his God. He knew something about this thing of "praying without ceasing." He knew something about constant communion and fellowship and the mighty power of God rested upon his life in an unbelievable way. God greatly used him to see thousands of people saved.

In Psalm 121:3 the Bible says, *"He that keepeth thee will not slumber."* That means there is never a bad time to call God. He is by the phone all the time.

How eager would you be, if you had a child on the

mission field, for the phone to ring? How eager would you be, if you could not see them, to hear their voice? How eager would you be if you could not spend physical, personal time with them, to commune with them on the phone? However eager you would be, multiply that by a thousand times and you might get a hold of the heart of God and how eager He is to hear from His people in good times and bad.

How many of you parents like to do things for your children? How many of you like it when they need you? I do. I want my kids to need me. That is part of human nature. We are made in the image of God, and it is part of God's nature, too. God wants to be needed.

You like to meet your children's needs, you love them, and you enjoy doing things for them. How many of you would be awfully disappointed if the only time your children ever got a hold of you was when they had a need? I want to meet their needs, but it is going to grieve my heart if they do not enjoy me, if they do not want to talk to me, if they do not really enjoy fellowship with me, if the only thing I am is a 911 number or a spare tire. It is going to grieve my heart. I am glad to meet their needs, but I want a relationship, not just to meet their needs. I do not want them to depend on someone else. I want them to depend on me. But I do not want them to ignore me and neglect me and reject me until they need. I would like to hear from them when things are going good. I would like to get in on the good news, too. I would like to hear from them just for some sweet fellowship.

That is the heart of God. God wants to hear from us. You will find the heart of God in Jeremiah 33:3. *"Call unto me, and I will answer thee, and shew thee great and mighty things, which thou knowest not."* We emphasize the last part of the verse, and we ought to, because the power of God is great. But we miss the heart of God. The heart of God is contained in the first few words. *"Call unto me."* If you do not need a miracle, *"Call unto me."* If you need a miracle, *"Call unto me,"* I have what you need. God wants that unbroken fellowship. God wants that unbroken communion. God wants that unbroken conversation.

Brother Hyles tells about when he was a young preacher, he stayed in a motel room for the first time with John Rice. Of course, he was awestruck with Dr. Rice, a great man of prayer.

He thought, "Boy, I am going to read about fifty chapters of my Bible tonight. I am going to pray for a couple of hours. That is what Dr. Rice is going to do when we get back to the room." He said Dr. Rice went into the bathroom, brushed his teeth, put on his pajamas, came back out, pulled the covers down, jumped into bed, pulled the covers up, looked to the right, looked to the left, and went straight to sleep. He never read a verse. He never prayed one word.

Brother Hyles was sitting over there befuddled. He did not know what to do. He was all ready to do all this reading and praying. So he went to bed, too.

The next morning they went to breakfast. He looked across the table at Dr. Rice and said, "Could I ask you a question?" He said, "Sure." "I thought surely last night before we went to sleep that you would spend some time in prayer." Old Dr. Rice said, "I was praying all day long. What were you doing?"

He was simply telling him, "I was in touch with heaven all day long. I shouldered the phone all day. I did not have any catching up to do at bed time. I did not have any getting a hold of God to do. I had a hold of Him all day long. It was time for me to rest. In my waking hours I never broke contact."

I have been gone from home for many days. If I could talk to my wife and kids as much as I would like to, I would just keep my phone on my shoulder all day long and talk to them. But I cannot afford that. My phone bill for business calls alone, without any fellowship on the phone, is usually over five hundred dollars a month. You know, I never have been billed from heaven. "You spent this much time in prayer. You have to pay this price." All I have ever received from heaven for my time spent in prayer are some pretty good dividend checks. I have received some pretty good blessings. It has never cost me. It has always paid. Everybody is always looking for ways to get ahead. That would be a good way to do it. It pays to pray. You may as well get God on the line in the morning and keep Him there all day long. It does not cost anything, and it does pay.

An old man named George Herbert, who passed off the scene many years ago, made this statement, "Prayer is the soul's blood." In Leviticus 17:11 the Bible says, *"The life of the flesh is in the blood."* If I do not have any blood, I am dead. What if my heart pumps for two hours in the morning, and it does not pump the rest of the day? How am I doing? Dead? Well, if prayer is the soul's blood, that means if I spend a half hour or fifteen minutes or an hour in the morning, and then I break contact and do not spend any time in prayer the rest of the day, how am I doing spiritually? Dead. I am not lost. I am not on my way to hell, but I have no zeal and I have no fervency and I have no discernment because I am not in touch with heaven.

I do not claim to be much of a Christian, but the truth I am talking about changed my life. It has helped me more than I can tell you. The tragedy to me is this. I believe that I probably spent more time in extemporaneous prayer today than some of you spent in planned prayer. Where does that put you?

I am supposed to pray while I study and pray while I drive. Some of the sweetest times I have with the Lord are at about three o'clock in the morning while I am driving down the road pulling our trailer. My wife and kids are all asleep. There is no one to talk to but Jesus. I have driven all night talking to the Lord about all kinds of things. He does not talk back out loud, but God gives me leadership in my heart and gives me peace about things. It is a sweet time. It is wonderful fellowship with the Lord.

This does not replace seasons of prayer. If you do not have planned prayer, if prayer is not important enough for you to have a set aside time, you will never carry on what you do not start. You will never continue what you do not establish. You have to have that morning time. It has to be important to you.

The absence of godly desire is a great problem in fundamentalism. But because of the absence of godly desire there is an absence of fervent prayer. There is an absence of real devotion to the person of God. I am not supposed to be after His. I am supposed to be after Him. My desire is not to be to His gifts. My desire is to be to Him.

When I got saved I was a barroom bouncer. I did not know any Bible verses. I would hear preachers say, "Walk with God. Walk with God." I said, "How do you do that? Where does He walk? How do you know if you are walking with Him?" I used to wonder about stuff like that. People said things but they did not tell me what they meant by it.

God is everywhere. He is not hard to find. For me to walk with God is for me to be joined with Him in prayer, and wherever I walk in communion with Him, I am walking with Him. To pray without ceasing is to walk with God.

Have you ever tried to call somebody and they were already on the line and you got a busy signal? The only thing worse than the fact that you got a busy signal and did not get through, is the fact that they do not even know that you tried to call.

Every day the devil is going to ring your number. But if you have God on the line, the devil is going to get a busy signal, and you will not even know that he called. Every day the world is going to ring your number, but if you have God on the line, the world is going to get a busy signal, and you will not even know that it tried to call. Every day the flesh is going to ring your number, but if you already have God on the line, the flesh is going to get a busy signal, and you will not even know that it tried to get in. Every day temptation is going to ring your number, and greed is going to ring your number, and lust is going to ring your number, and jealousy is going to ring your number, and depression is going to ring your number, and bitterness will ring your number, and laziness will ring your number, and indifference will ring your number, but if you get God on the line in the morning and never break the connection, and keep the phone on your shoulder the rest of the day, all of those things that should not get into your mind will not get anything but a busy signal. You will not even know that they tried to get in.

The problem is, some of you have call waiting. Call waiting is of the devil! You get God on the line and you are doing pretty good. Then something happens and you say, "Just a minute, Lord. Hello? I will be right back, flesh, just give me a minute to get the Lord off the line. Lord, I got a call. See you later."

God wants us to get Him on the line and keep Him on the line in unbroken fellowship, all day long. It will protect you. If you pray without ceasing it will keep you from panicking and making a bad decision. It will keep you from fainting or quitting, throwing in the towel. It will keep you from dying spiritually. It will keep you from being torn up about everything that happens. It will keep you from getting the bad things into your mind that should not get there. It will keep you from losing your joy. It will affect every part of your life.

True Christianity is a walk with God. If I am walking with Him, He is going to walk me by some people who are lost. He is going to give me something to do to serve Him. He is going to empower me as I do it.

It is not a matter of idleness, where I walk around in a daze talking to God, and I do not have any useful purpose in life. God said, "I want you to be useful, but I do not want you to hang up on Me while you are doing the work I have given you to do. I want you to get Me on the phone in the morning and shoulder the phone the rest of the day."

Morning prayer is kind of like going out and starting your car and warming it up. When you start your car, what do you start it for? Do you intend to go somewhere with it? Suppose you go out and start your car up, and whenever you get it warm, you shut it off and walk. That is not too smart. But that is what you do in prayer. You get alone with God and spend a half hour with Him, or spend an hour with Him, and you pray. Then you say, "Okay, see You, Lord." You take off on your own. He says, "Wait a minute. What do you think this morning time was for? This was to get things warmed up. I want to stay in contact the rest of the day."

If you started your car, I imagine you intended to back it out of the driveway and take it. If you are going to have a morning prayer time, you ought to go ahead and keep the phone shouldered and keep in touch with God all day long. You do not have to hang up. He said, *"Pray without ceasing."*

If I am going to do that, first of all, I have to schedule a morning prayer time. I have to be serious enough to set aside a time when I am going to get a hold of God.

I am not going to tell you what makes you spiritual, how many minutes or hours, or what time you have to get up to be spiritual. That does not have a thing to do with it. Start the day with God. Begin with Him. Set something reasonable that you can live with, but something that is real. Then, when you get through with your prayer time, scheduled, on purpose, designated, shoulder the phone the rest of the day. Do not hang up on Him. End your prayer with a comma or a semicolon, and stay in touch with God all day long.

IF YOU WERE TO DIE TODAY, ARE YOU 100% SURE THAT YOU WOULD GO TO HEAVEN? If you could know that, you would want to, wouldn't you? Please take a few moments and let me share with you how the Bible says that you can know...

"Wherefore, as by one man sin entered into the world, an death by sin: and so death passed upon all men, for that all have sinned:" *(Romans 5:12)* The one thing that stands between us and going to Heaven when we die is our sin --- and God said that ALL have sinned. He didn't leave anyone out. If I'm going to be honest with myself, I must admit that I am included. I am a sinner first of all because I inherited a sinful nature from Adam that has been passed down to me. I am a sinner because I have disobeyed the clear commands of God. Just as it only takes one instance of stealing to make me a thief, it takes only one sin to make me a sinner. There are no 'good sinners' or 'bad sinners' in the eyes of God --- we all stand guilty before Him, and unworthy of Heaven.

The Bible says that there is a penalty for sin --- DEATH. *"...and so death passed upon all men, for that all have sinned."* *(Romans 5:12) "for the wages of sin is death..."* *(Romans 6:23)* You cannot pay for sin by going to church or being baptized or doing good deeds or keeping commandments. The only payment that will clear your account is death. This is not just a physical death. They Bible is clear that after the body dies, there is a second death or a spiritual death.

"But the fearful, and unbelieving, and the

abominable, and murderers, and whoremongers, and sorcerers, and idolaters, and all liars, shall have their part in the lake which burneth with fire and brimstone which is the second death." *(Revelation 21:8)* The Bible is clear that if we must pay the price for our sin, we must suffer a second death forever in the lake of fire called hell. No other payment that we can make would pay the price, because the wages of sin is death.

God loves us so much that He did not want us to go to hell, even though we deserve to do so. Yet he would not be just and righteous if He allowed us to go to Heaven with our sin, just as a judge would be unjust to let a murderer go free just because it was someone he knew and loved. Sin must be paid for. There is only one way for our sin to be paid for without you and I spending all eternity in the torment of Hell: to let Someone else pay the price for us.

"For God so loved the world, that he gave his only begotten Son, that whosoever believeth in him should not perish, but have everlasting life." *(John 3:16)* God allowed His Son, Jesus Christ, to suffer and die in our place to pay the price of death that we owe. We do not need to do anything to earn it, we must simply receive the salvation that Jesus paid for with His blood. *"But as many as received him, to them gave he power to become the sons of God, even to them that believe on his name:"* *(John 1:12)* If we will receive Jesus and His death on the cross as payment for our sins, He has promised to receive us into His family as a child of God.

"Behold, I stand at the door, and knock: if any man hear my voice, and open the door, I will come in to him..." *(Revelation 3:20)* Receiving Christ is as simple as opening the door and inviting someone in. Christ stands ready to come into your heart, forgive your sins, and make you a child of God. But he will only come by invitation. Won't you bow your head right now, wherever you are, and invite

the Lord Jesus Christ to come in?

Lord Jesus,
I know that I am a sinner, and that I deserve to go to hell. Please forgive me and come into my heart right now. I'm trusting you to make me a child of God, to take me to Heaven when I die, and to help me live the rest of my life for you. Thank you for saving me.
In Jesus' name, Amen

If you sincerely prayed that prayer and asked the Lord to save you, He said, ***"...I will come in."*** That's not a maybe. He promised that He would. If you died right now with Christ in your heart where would you go? To Heaven! If you had died before you asked Christ into your heart, where would you have gone? The difference between heaven and hell is the Lord Jesus Christ living within, Who died to pay the price of our sin.

Now that Christ lives in your heart, He has promised that He will never leave. ***"...for he hath said, I will never leave thee, nor forsake thee."*** No matter when you die, Christ will still be in your heart as He promised, so Heaven is as sure as if you were already there.

God does expect us to obey Him after we become His children, and the very first command that He gives is found in Acts 2:38. ***"...Repent, and be baptized every one of you..."*** Repentance takes place within, when I turn away from sin and self and turn to Christ as my Savior. Baptism is the outward sign of what has happened in my heart --- a picture of the death, burial and resurrection of Jesus. Immediately after we get saved, God expects us to be baptized and show the world that we belong to Him.

If you have received Christ into your heart as a result of reading Revival Fires!, please write and let us know. We'd like to send you a free copy of GROWING UP IN GOD'S

FAMILY and LIVING UP TO YOUR NAME.

_____

Name

_____

Address

_____

City, State, Zip

_____

Phone Number

Send to:
Dennis Corle Evangelistic Assoc. -- Revival Fires!
P.O. Box 245, Claysburg, PA 16625
(814) 239-2813